Cindy Kendall

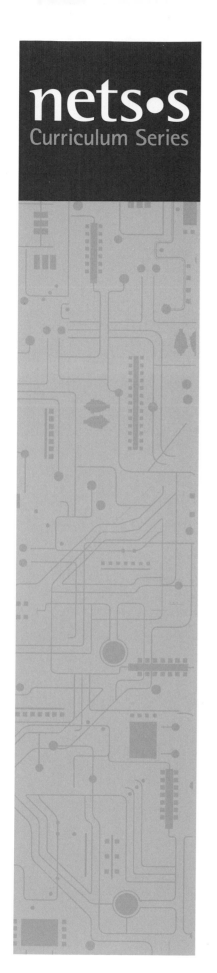

nets·s
Curriculum Series

National Educational Technology
Standards for Students

Multidisciplinary Units
for Grades 3–5

D0862474

iste

nets•s
Curriculum Series

Multidisciplinary Units for Grades 3–5

DIRECTOR OF PUBLISHING
Jean Marie Hall

EDITOR
Larry Hannah

COPY EDITOR
Kellee Weinhold

BOOK DESIGN
Katherine Getta,
Katherine Getta Graphic Design

LAYOUT AND PRODUCTION
Tracy Cozzens

AQUISITIONS EDITORS
Anita McAnear
Mathew Manweller

BOOK PUBLISHING PROJECT MANAGER
Tracy Cozzens

DATA AND COMMUNICATIONS MANAGER
Diannah Anavir

ADMINISTRATIVE ASSISTANT
Pam Calegari

International Society for Technology in Education (ISTE)
480 Charnelton Street
Eugene, OR 97401-2626
Order Desk: 1.800.336.5191
Order Fax: 541.302.3778
Customer Service: orders@iste.org
Books and Courseware: books@iste.org
World Wide Web: www.iste.org

First Edition
ISBN 1-56484-176-6

about
iste

The International Society for Technology in Education (ISTE) is a nonprofit professional organization with a worldwide membership of leaders in educational technology. We are dedicated to promoting appropriate uses of information technology to support and improve learning, teaching, and administration in K–12 education and teacher education. As part of that mission, ISTE provides high-quality and timely information, services, and materials, such as this book.

ISTE's Publishing Department works with experienced educators to develop and produce classroom-tested books and courseware. We look for content that emphasizes the use of technology where it can make a difference—making the teacher's job easier; saving time; motivating students; helping students who have unique learning styles, abilities, or backgrounds; and creating learning environments that would be impossible without technology. We believe technology can improve the effectiveness of teaching while making learning exciting and fun.

Every manuscript and product we select for publication is peer reviewed and professionally edited. While we take pride in our publications, we also recognize the difficulties of maintaining quality while keeping on top of the latest technologies and research. Please let us know what products you would find helpful. We value your feedback on this book and other ISTE products. E-mail us at books@iste.org.

ISTE is home of the National Educational Technology Standards (NETS) Project and the National Center for Preparing Tomorrow's Teachers to Use Technology (NCPT3). To learn more about NETS or request a print catalog, visit our Web site at www.iste.org, which provides:

- Current educational technology standards for K–12 student and teacher education
- A bookstore with online ordering and membership discount options
- Learning & Leading with Technology magazine
- ISTE Update, membership newsletter
- Teacher resources
- Discussion groups
- Professional development services, including national conference information
- Research projects
- Member services

Senior Editor

LARRY HANNAH
Pioneer Learning and Emeritus Professor of Teacher Education, California State University, Sacramento

Larry Hannah has taught at the University level for more than 30 years. He established the educational technology program at CSUS and has seen it grow into an highly successful, dynamic offering. Larry's special areas of interest include applications of teaching strategies to on- and off-line instruction and developing leadership skills with technology-using teachers, curriculum developers and administrators.

Co-Editors

MIKE MENCHACA is an assistant professor of Teacher Education at California State University, Sacramento. His areas of focus include learning online, community-based learning, staff development, graduate programs, and technology standards. He has collaborated and consulted with K–12 schools, districts, and county offices. He is currently finishing his doctorate at Pepperdine University in Malibu, California.

BRUCE MCVICKER has taught for public elementary and secondary schools in the United States and Australia for 27 years. Bruce specializes in teaching problem solving using databases and spreadsheets. He uses web-based learning as an effective way to integrate the curriculum with new technologies. Bruce is currently the CSUS Teacher in Residence and in the final year of his doctoral studies at the University of California, Davis specializing in School Organization and Education Policy.

Contributing Authors

DEBORAH AUFDENSPRING is a classroom teacher and consultant who conducts workshops in project-based learning and in integrating technology into curricula. She also has made many presentations around the country about her innovative humanities curriculum. She was one of the teachers who opened New Technology High School in Napa, California, and after teaching there for its first four years, moved to Minnesota to help open the Minnesota Business Academy in Saint Paul. The next school she is helping start is the Mare Island Technology Academy High School in Vallejo, California.

MITCH HALL has been using educational technology since tin cans and string were high tech in the classroom. He has been a classroom teacher, technology resource teacher, staff development coordinator, and he is currently director of Instructional Technology and Learning Resources for the Sacramento County Office of Education. Mitch enjoys travel, nature photography, mountain biking, and learning the blues harmonica. He and his wife live in the Sierra Nevadas east of Sacramento, California.

HEATHER HOFFMAN is a third-grade teacher in the Roseville City School District. She teaches at Woodbridge Fundamental School, a Title I school with a high English

Language Learner population. Heather has taught for 13 years. For the past five years, she has been a technology trainer of trainers at her site. Heather also has presented at the Technology Reading and Learning Disability International Conference and the Cap CUE conference. These presentations showed how to incorporate technology into the curriculum. In the past, she has been a collaborative teacher for California State University, Sacramento. For the past three years, she has participated in a grant called Preparing Tomorrow's Teachers to use Technology, developing curriculum units that incorporate technology. She is working toward a master's degree in Educational Technology.

RONI JONES has been a classroom teacher for 10 years, teaching fourth and sixth grades. She earned her master's degree in education from California State University, Sacramento, where she is serving as project director of a federally funded grant program, "Preparing Tomorrow's Teachers to use Technology." Since 1995, she has been actively involved in the California Geographic Alliance and, for the past two summers, has edited curricula and trained teachers to use "Mission Geography," produced by Texas A&M University and NASA.

MAUREEN MCMAHON is a science educator with 15 years of experience teaching science and technology courses in K–12 schools and science and technology education courses at the post-secondary level. She received her Ph.D. in science education from Maryland in 1994. She teaches elementary science methods at California State University, Long Beach, where she chairs the Department of Science Education. Her research includes investigations into how teachers use technology in their lesson planning and teaching.

WALTER MCKENZIE is a teacher, trainer, and consultant who has been incorporating technology and multiple intelligences theory into instruction throughout the past decade. He serves as chair of the Department of Instruction at Connected University, an online professional development community, where he taught a class on Teaching Multiple Intelligences through Technology. He also gives presentations on multiple intelligences, technology integration, and creative education around the country. He hosts an education Web site titled The One and Only Surfaquarium (**http://surfaquarium.com**) and his Innovative Teaching weekly newsletter has 2,800 subscribers. He is as an instructional technology coordinator for Arlington Public Schools in Virginia.

SUSAN O'HARA received her bachelor's degree in mathematics and physics from University College Dublin in Ireland. She moved with her family to the United States and completed a master of arts degree in statistics at the University of Southern California in Los Angeles. She earned a Ph.D. in September 2000 from the University of California, Davis, in mathematics, science, and technology education, and is now an assistant professor of Teacher Education at California State University, Sacramento. O'Hara is interested in the role of the teacher in effective science, mathematics, and technology reform, the use of technology as a vehicle for providing all students with meaningful learning experiences, and the development of effective professional development models that facilitate an infusion of technology into curricula.

LINDA PERRY works for the California Technology Assistance Project, Region 3, at the Sacramento County Office of Education where she coordinates technology projects in elementary and adult education and technology integration. She has worked as a first- through sixth-grade computer resource teacher. Her students frequently created projects similar to the ones described in Theme 1—Form and Structure, in Chapter 3. She also took part in teaching exchanges in Montreal and Quebec, Canada.

contents

introduction

The NETS Project

The National Educational Technology Standards (NETS) Project was initiated by the International Society for Technology in Education's Accreditation and Professional Standards Committee. ISTE has emerged as a recognized leader among professional organizations for educators involved with technology. ISTE's mission is to promote appropriate uses of technology to support and improve learning, teaching, and administration. Its members are leaders in educational technology, including teachers, technology coordinators, education administrators, and teacher educators. ISTE supports all subject area disciplines by providing publications, conferences, online resources, and services that help educators combine the knowledge and skills of their teaching fields with the application of technologies to improve learning and teaching.

The primary goal of the NETS Project is to enable stakeholders in PK–12 education to develop national standards for the educational uses of technology that facilitate school improvement in the United States. The NETS Project is developing standards to guide educational leaders in recognizing and addressing the essential conditions for effective use of technology to support PK–12 education.

The NETS•S Curriculum Series project represents a continuation of ISTE's desire to provide educators with the means to meet the NETS standards. Multidisciplinary Units for Grades 3–5 is specifically designed to provide elementary teachers with curriculum in order to meet the grade level 3–5 Performance Indicators of the NETS standards.

NATIONAL EDUCATIONAL TECHNOLOGY STANDARDS FOR STUDENTS

The National Educational Technology Standards (NETS) for students are divided into six broad categories. Standards within each category are to be introduced, reinforced, and mastered by students. These categories provide a framework for linking performance indicators, listed by grade level, to the standards. Teachers can use these standards and profiles as guidelines for planning technology-based activities in which students achieve success in learning, communication, and life skills.

1. **Basic operations and concepts**
   - Students demonstrate a sound understanding of the nature and operation of technology systems.
   - Students are proficient in the use of technology.

2. **Social, ethical, and human issues**
   - Students understand the ethical, cultural, and societal issues related to technology.
   - Students practice responsible use of technology systems, information, and software.

- Students develop positive attitudes toward technology uses that support lifelong learning, collaboration, personal pursuits, and productivity.

3. Technology productivity tools

- Students use technology tools to enhance learning, increase productivity, and promote creativity.

- Students use productivity tools to collaborate in constructing technology-enhanced models, preparing publications, and producing other creative works.

4. Technology communications tools

- Students use telecommunications to collaborate, publish, and interact with peers, experts, and other audiences.

- Students use a variety of media and formats to communicate information and ideas effectively to multiple audiences.

5. Technology research tools

- Students use technology to locate, evaluate, and collect information from a variety of sources.

- Students use technology tools to process data and report results.

- Students evaluate and select new information resources and technological innovations based on the appropriateness to specific tasks.

6. Technology problem-solving and decision-making tools

- Students use technology resources for solving problems and making informed decisions.

- Students employ technology in the development of strategies for solving problems in the real world.

PROFILES FOR TECHNOLOGY-LITERATE STUDENTS (GRADES 3-5)

All students should have opportunities to demonstrate the following performances. Numbers in parentheses following each performance indicator refer to the standards category to which the performance is linked. ISTE has developed Performance Indicators for all grade levels. However, below are listed only the Grades 3-5 indicators—the specific focus of this book.

Prior to completion of Grade 5 students will

- use keyboards and other common input and output devices (including adaptive devices when necessary) efficiently and effectively. (1)

- discuss common uses of technology in daily life and the advantages and disadvantages those uses provide. (1, 2)

- discuss basic issues related to responsible use of technology and information and describe personal consequences of inappropriate use. (2)

- use general purpose productivity tools and peripherals to support personal productivity, remediate skill deficits, and facilitate learning throughout the curriculum. (3)

- use technology tools (e.g., multimedia authoring and presentation software, Web tools, digitalcameras, scanners) for individual and collaborative writing, communicating and publishing activities to create knowledge products for audiences inside and outside the classroom. (3, 4)

- use telecommunications efficiently and effectively to access remote information, communicate with others in support of direct and independent learning, and pursue personal interests. (4)

- use telecommunications and online resources (e.g., e-mail, online discussions, Web environments) to participate in collaborative problem-solving activities for the purpose of developing solutions or products for audiences inside and outside the classroom. (4, 5)

- use technology resources (e.g., calculators, data collection probes, videos, and educational software) in activities for problem-solving, self-directed learning, and extended learning. (5, 6)

- determine when technology is useful and select the appropriate tool(s) and technology resources to address a variety of tasks and problems. (5, 6)

- evaluate the accuracy, relevance, appropriateness, comprehensiveness, and bias of electronic information sources. (6)

Section 2 provides resource units divided into five themes. This technology-embedded curriculum is specifically designed to help students meet the above performance indicators.

Essential Conditions for Technology Integration

Successful learning activities, such as the ones provided in this book, depend on more than just the technology. Certain conditions are necessary for schools to effectively use technology for learning, teaching, and educational management. Physical, human, financial, and policy dimensions greatly affect the success of technology use in schools.

The curriculum provided in this book will be more effective if a combination of essential conditions to create learning environments conducive to powerful uses of technology are met, including:

- vision with support and proactive leadership from the education system;
- educators skilled in the use of technology for learning;
- content standards and curriculum resources;
- student-centered approaches to learning;
- assessment of the effectiveness of technology for learning;
- access to contemporary technologies, software, and telecommunications networks;
- technical assistance for maintaining and using technology resources;
- community partners who provide expertise, support, and real-life interactions;
- ongoing financial support for sustained technology use; and
- policies and standards supporting new learning environments.

Traditional educational practices no longer provide students with all the necessary skills for economic survival in today's workplace. Students today must apply strategies for solving problems using appropriate tools for learning, collaborating, and communicating. The following chart lists characteristics representing traditional approaches to learning and corresponding strategies associated with new learning environments:

ESTABLISHING NEW LEARNING ENVIRONMENTS

Incorporating New Strategies

Traditional Learning Environments ⟶ New Learning Environments

Traditional Learning Environments	New Learning Environments
Teacher-centered instruction	Student-centered learning
Single-sense stimulation	Multisensory stimulation
Single-path progression	Multipath progression
Single media	Multimedia
Isolated work	Collaborative work
Information delivery	Information exchange
Passive learning	Active/exploratory/inquiry-based learning
Factual, knowledge-based learning	Critical thinking and informed decision-making
Reactive response	Proactive/planned action
Isolated, artificial context	Authentic, real-world context

The most effective learning environments meld traditional approaches and new approaches to facilitate learning of relevant content while addressing individual needs. The resulting learning environments should prepare students to:

- communicate using a variety of media and formats;
- access and exchange information in a variety of ways;
- compile, organize, analyze, and synthesize information;
- draw conclusions and make generalizations based on information gathered;
- know content and be able to locate additional information as needed;
- become self-directed learners;
- collaborate and cooperate in team efforts; and
- interact with others in ethical and appropriate ways.

Teachers know that the wise use of technology can enrich learning environments and enable students to achieve marketable skills. We hope that elementary educators will find the curriculum and other material provided within helpful in meeting these goals.

How to Use This Book

NETS•S Curriculum Series—Multidisciplinary Units for Grades 3-5 is divided into two main sections followed by a set of useful appendixes.

Section 1 provides a series of pieces that will help teachers successfully integrate technology into an elementary classroom. Teachers are provided with strategies on how to incorporate technology into a one-computer classroom, multi-computer classroom or a classroom that utilizes a computer lab. Teachers are also given ideas on how to use cooperative teaching strategies, how to develop problem-based learning activities, and how to incorporate responsible and effective use of the Internet into the classroom.

Section 2 provides teachers with five multidisciplinary curriculum Themes containing resource units. Each Theme has a unique topic (Form and Structure, Imagination, Perspectives, Movement, and Change). In addition to a host of long- and short-term lesson plans, each unit offers seven Unit Tools. These Unit Tools consist of:

SPOTLIGHT ON TECHNOLOGY: Each unit highlights the use of one or more types of technology. For example, the Imagination Unit focuses on Web page construction and editing digital movies. The Spotlight on Technology section explains how the highlighted technology can be incorporated into a variety of different lesson plans that teachers may want to design in the future.

CHILDREN'S LITERATURE: All of the Units in this book focus on a multidisciplinary approach to teaching. Because reading and writing are so important, each Unit offers a list of books teachers may want to use in conjunction with the lesson provided.

WRITING ACROSS THE CURRICULUM: This "tool" is provided for teachers who are looking for writing extension assignments. In each Unit, the Writing Across the Curriculum section offers a variety of essay topics and writing assignments that can be added to the lessons provided.

TEACHER VOICES: Teachers want to know what other teachers think. This section provides the reader with feedback from other teachers.

WEB RESOURCES: Many of the Units expect that students have access to the Web. The Web Resources "tool" gives the teacher a list of important Web sites that can be used to enhance the provided lessons.

TEACHING TIPS: It always helps to have suggestions on the best way to implement a lesson. The Teaching Tips "tool" suggests ways in which a teacher can get the most out of the lessons. This section provides insights into which teaching strategy might be most effective for you.

LESSON EXTENDERS: Sometimes lessons are so good, students and teachers don't want them to end. If that is the case with some of the lessons provided, each Unit offers a few suggestions for lesson extensions.

The *Appendixes* provide several additional resources for the teacher. Included are content area standards and sample assessment rubrics.

Beyond This Book

Keep in mind that the authors of individual learning activities could not address the needs of every teaching situation. Take the examples contained herein and modify them to fit your circumstances and needs. The sample lessons also provide a lens for re-examining traditional lessons and discovering ways to infuse technology to enrich teaching and learning. As you are inspired to create new lessons and units, please share these with others by posting them on the ISTE Web site (www.iste.org). But that's not all!

Be proactive about sharing your good work with others. There are many lesson plan Web sites as well as school, district, professional association, and parent meetings at which to present new lesson plans and the resulting student work. Educators need to learn from their peers. Educators also need to inform parents of their efforts to integrate technology and learning; and inform the greater public about how schools are meeting the needs of students, parents, and the community.

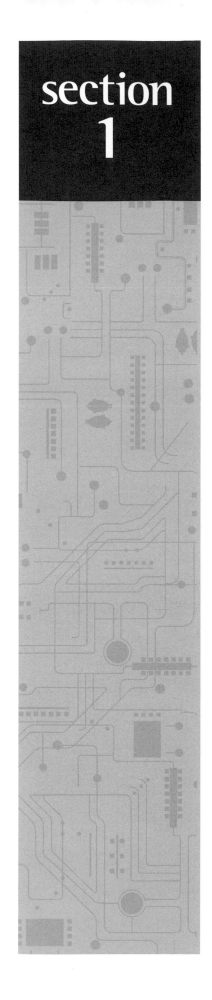

section 1

Strategies for Getting Started

chapter 1

BY SUSAN O'HARA

Using Technology in Different Settings

How Many Computers Do You Have?

Multiple-computer classrooms are becoming more and more commonplace. However, many teachers have only one computer in the classroom or access to a computer lab and no computers in the classroom. Whichever of these settings you are using, it is very important that students see technology as a tool for learning, not as an add-on separate from the curriculum. Teachers and students should work together to bring technology into the central activities in their classrooms and make computers available to all students. Technology should be a central component of the curriculum and is most effective when used in constructivist, problem-based learning environments. In an online article on the most powerful models of instruction, the North Central Regional Educational Laboratory (NCREL) discusses actively engaging the learner when integrating technology into the curriculum.

The most powerful models of instruction are interactive. Instruction actively engages the learner, and is generative. Instruction encourages the learner to construct and produce knowledge in meaningful ways. Students teach others interactively and interact generatively with their teachers and peers. This allows for co-construction of knowledge, which promotes engaged learning that is problem-, project-, and goal-based. Some common strategies included in engaged learning models of instruction are individual and group summarizing, means of exploring multiple perspectives, techniques for building upon prior knowledge, brainstorming, Socratic dialogue, problem-solving processes, and team teaching, according to NCREL.

The following chapter provides strategies and ideas for effectively infusing technology into constructivist, problem-based classrooms in different technology settings.

Cooperative Learning Group

Afternoons in Mr. Thomas's classroom are dedicated to project time. During project time, the four computers in the classroom become a part of four centers: a research center, a scanning and digital art center, a data collection and analysis center, and a presentation center.

Rather than teach each of his students how to use all of these stations effectively, Mr. Thomas has decided to use a peer-coaching model. He divides his class into four teams and trains each team to be experts for one of the centers. One team becomes expert at conducting research online and using search engines. A second team learns effective strategies for scanning, editing images, creating images, and using a paint and draw program. The third team focuses on entering, sorting, and finding data in a database, and on analyzing the data once it is entered. The last team learns how to create effective presentations using a program such as PowerPoint.

As Mr. Thomas works with each team, the focus is not simply on the technology skills, but also on effective application of these skills. Once each team has spent time mastering a specialty, Mr. Thomas restructures the groups so that each new group now has at least one expert for each of the centers. The new groups begin working on a project. As they rotate through the centers working on projects, all students mentor each other at each of the centers, assuming the role of expert or novice depending on their expertise.

The vignette above illustrates a model for setting up cooperative groups to work in a six-computer classroom. Cooperative learning groups are essential components of constructivist learning environments. In addition, they facilitate using technology effectively in any computer setting. It is very important to set up these groups so that students' time spent on task is most effective. Research shows that one way to do this is to set up heterogeneous groups where knowledge and expertise can be shared.

Collaborative work that is learning-centered often involves small groups or teams of two or more students within a classroom or across classroom boundaries. Heterogeneous groups (including different sexes, cultures, abilities, ages, and socioeconomic backgrounds) offer a wealth of background knowledge and perspectives to different tasks. Flexible grouping, which allows teachers to reconfigure small groups according to the purposes of instruction and incorporates frequent heterogeneous groups, is one of the most equitable means of grouping and ensuring increased learning opportunities.

Setting up Centers

The students in Ms. Collins' fourth-grade class have been working together on a unit focusing on environmental issues. The class is working in six teams of four. Each team has chosen a different environmental issue to focus the team's project on and is required to conduct some research on the topic and create a multimedia presentation. On this morning, students are working in their teams to complete their projects.

Ms. Collins has set up six different centers in the classroom. At one corner of the room, there are a number of encyclopedias and books related to the project topic for teams to conduct some of their research. The team that is working at this center on Wednesday morning is reading about pollution and making notes about the research. The students are also planning the additional information they will research online when they go to the computer center.

A table, some chairs, and some art materials make up a second center, where a team of students is working on the importance of recycling. They are designing illustrated signs for recycling, which they plan to scan into the computer at a later time and post around their school.

Center three has literature and poetry books related to the topic. The team at this center is sitting on some beanbags in a circle reading The Lorax *and discussing its relevance to their project.*

Center four is a discussion area for teams to plan and update their progress periodically. On this day, the students of one team are sitting at the discussion area debating whether they should conduct a survey of their peers to determine their feelings about saving more trees. They decide that they could input the data into the computer at a later time and graph the results.

At another corner of the room is the computer station with a printer and scanner where a team of students is researching the effects of acid rain. They are online trying to answer some of the questions they had brainstormed at the discussion center.

At center six, there is a table and some chairs, where students can write. The team at this center is composing a persuasive letter to a company to provide the company with some strategies for making the company more environmentally friendly.

All students work for approximately an hour at these centers and then they rotate to the next center. On the wall is a schedule that the teacher has posted and that lists the times each team will be at each center. As the teams work through the five-week unit they rotate through the centers, until each group has spent time at each of the centers.

The above vignette illustrates how one teacher used centers in her one-computer classroom. Centers are a wonderful way to maximize use of computers in the one- or multiple-computer classroom. Centers also allow students to be to understand the different tools and resources they might use when conducting research or completing projects. If the centers include multiple resources, which are not all computer-based, students begin to understand that computers are another tool for learning.

In the one-computer classroom, teachers can use the computer as a research center, keeping multimedia encyclopedias, tools such as dictionaries and spreadsheets, and Internet access readily available to students on an as-needed basis. Having students use the technology at one center and other means of researching and presenting at other centers reinforces the idea of the technology as a tool for learning. In classrooms where centers are used, the computer can be used as a learning center. For example, the computer can be used as a research center, a data collection center, a statistical analysis center, a multimedia center, or a presentation center.

In the multiple-computer classroom, students centers are also very effective. Teams can sometimes work on the same activity or computers can be part of different centers for different uses. For example, in a five-computer classroom you could have one computer as part of a reading and research center, a writing center, an art center, a data collection and analysis center, and a presentation center. Just like in the one-computer classroom, students rotate through the centers until each team has spent time at each center. You can also combine this with the cooperative group model by training each student to be an expert for one of the centers and allowing the student to facilitate peer learning as they work at that center.

Scheduling Rotations

Ms. Jones teaches fifth grade. In her classroom there is one computer. Ms. Jones uses the computer in two different ways, to facilitate both individual work and group work. To help students with their basic computer skills, such as keyboarding, using the mouse, and navigating the computer, she sets up a rotation schedule for all mornings a week in her classroom.

During this time, while the class is working on reading and computational skills, a student is pulled out for 15 minutes to work on the computer, then the next student rotates in and this continues for the entire morning. In this way, each student has access to the computers for basic skill development for 15 minutes each week. This schedule is different each week so students don't always miss the same instructional period.

To accommodate group work, Ms. Jones allows her students to have access to the computers during free time in the afternoon and she posts a rotation schedule next to the computer. By using this method Ms. Jones can allow two to three different groups of students to work on the computer in one day.

Teachers should have a class schedule posted where students rotate at 15-minute shifts all day, even during direct instruction. Because they are in the classroom while working on their assignments, they still hear all the necessary instruction. Well-planned schedules allow all students to have equal amounts of time on the computer, both for development of individual skills and for research and project work. It also makes use of the students in your class who are tech-savvy. Many students love computers and have strong problem-solving and trouble-shooting skills. Allow these students to assist when other students are working on the computers in your classroom. Scheduling time for these students to coach others in the class about computer trouble-shooting is a very good idea. In the process, they develop valuable expertise. Let them explore new software, teach you how to use it, tutor classmates, and trouble-shoot.

Sharing Resources

At King Elementary School, several fourth- and fifth-grade teachers work as a team to write a grant that will supply the school with a mobile cart and 30 laptops that have wireless access. They receive the grant and begin working collaboratively to decide how to divide the time and create a schedule for using the computers in their classrooms.

While discussing these issues, the teachers plan how they might use the computers in their classroom and infuse the technology into their curriculum. Many of the teachers identify commonalities in the projects they are working on with their students. As they spend more time planning, they see ways they could have their students work together on projects and ways they could integrate across subject areas to make these projects even richer.

As a team, the teachers develop some integrated units that are infused with technology. One teacher is an expert with using databases, another with Web authoring, and yet another with a draw and paint program. They decide that they can teach and support each other by sharing their knowledge and skills. They build a schedule for their integrated units and for use of the mobile computer lab. Excited about the use of this new technology and by the newfound collaboration, they decide to pilot the units in the new year and to continue to work as a team to update and refine their units.

Another useful way of maximizing the benefit of few computers in the school, while still allowing teachers to use the computers within the classroom setting, is to have a mobile cart with laptops that can be shared among teachers at different times in the day. Wireless access allows this mobile cart to become a computer lab complete with Internet access and e-mail access, which can be shared among groups of teachers and still be purchased at a reasonable cost. Working with other teachers to plan and create a schedule for use is essential when sharing resources. An added benefit to this type of collaboration is that teachers can also share curriculum ideas for working with computers.

Using the Computer Lab

Mr. Barter has no computers in his fourth-grade classroom. He does, however, have access to a computer lab that houses 30 computers with Internet access, two printers, a scanner, and a presentation station. Mr. Barter's fourth-grade class is working on a project in which they are exploring inventions and inventors from the 1800s. In pairs the students have chosen an invention or inventor to study. Their culminating project is to create a final illustrated report and accompanying multimedia presentation on their chosen topic.

Mr. Barter's class has access to the computer lab one afternoon a week for two hours. The students are working on their projects two afternoons a week; one two-hour session is in class, the second two-hour session is in the lab. During the class time, students use books and encyclopedias in their classroom or go to the library to conduct research there. Students brainstorm questions they will need to research online and compile a list of these questions. They also put together an action plan for their time in the computer lab.

Following a schedule made by Mr. Barter, pairs of students spend time working with the scanner so that all teams have equal amounts of time for scanning images. In addition, students spend the class project time handwriting and editing drafts of the written portion of their projects and storyboarding their final presentations. Each student pair creates a draft of the multimedia presentation on a set of index cards in which each card represents a slide.

Once students go to the lab they have a well-structured plan of action. On any afternoon when students are working in the lab, they can be found researching on the Internet, scanning in images and handwritten documents, typing their reports using a word processing program, or working on their multimedia projects. When all the projects have been created, students use the presentation station in the lab.

For teachers with no computers in the classroom but access to a computer lab, planning is very important. Students should be taught to see the computers as an integral part of what they are learning and as a resource for their schoolwork. Teachers should make sure that students plan their time in the lab in advance. Also, it is important to use a schedule to ensure that all students have equal access to the resources the computer lab provides. With a block of time in the computer lab, can be used very effectively at centers within the lab. Computer labs can be designed to include large tables for work at away from the computers. When deciding on how the lab should be configured, teachers and the technology support staff should discuss the different options. In addition, collaborating with the other teachers to create a schedule for the lab and discuss the different ways it can be used is very important and can lead to some fruitful partnerships among the teachers.

Conclusion

Even in classrooms where students and teachers have limited access to computers, groups of students can use technology in very effective ways. One of the key components of an effective use of instructional technology in the classroom is careful planning. Collaborating and sharing resources with the other people is very helpful and often leads to new ideas for using technology in the classroom. In addition, different organizations and corporations offer schools a number of grants and funding opportunities. Putting together a grant writing team is a good idea to help increase the technology available to teachers and to provide training for those teachers. While this chapter offers strategies for using technology in a variety of settings, it is also important to think ahead to new ways of adding technology resources.

chapter 2

BY DEBORAH AUFDENSPRING

Project- and Problem-Based Learning

Watching project- and problem-based learning take place in a classroom underscores its significant differences from usual classroom practices. One might see small groups of students talking quietly, laughing, or practicing a presentation. Others might be hunched over computer screens discussing the data displayed on the screen, or students might move among groups discussing common issues. It may even be difficult to find the teacher as she melds into a group of students, making suggestions but not directing their activities. Rarely in such a classroom are students playing at their desks, passing notes, falling asleep, or asking for passes out of the room. Rather, most of the students are relaxed and yet maintain an attentive seriousness—an attitude that this is real work, deserving of respectful attention. Such behavior is the result of teachers who keep reading and lecturing to a minimum in favor of more compelling activities. Some teachers even forgo traditional testing modes, relying solely on students' projects for assessment.

The philosophical and research-based underpinnings of project- and problem-based learning follow the constructivist theories of Piaget, Dewey, Bruner, and Taba. Project-based learning clearly creates the conditions for students to take charge of their own learning and create their own knowledge from a great variety of sources of information.

Project- and problem-based learning can be considered two ends of a spectrum of constructivist learning. In project-based learning, conditions may be more clearly delineated than in problem-based learning, but they still leave students with wide latitude for determining the course of their learning. Problem-based learning is messier and asks students to reformulate their hypotheses in the midst of solving a problem.

What Is Project-Based Learning?

Project-based learning is a model for teaching that focuses on the major concepts of a curriculum, involving students in meaningful investigations of those concepts. Concepts may be introduced by a teacher and supported by texts, speakers, and other sources. Students then work autonomously to create projects that demonstrate their learning to teachers, peers, and the community.

CONTENT

Compelling and complex ideas and projects are presented to students are in turn required to deal with ambiguity. These problems are real-world problems that students care about; the problems presented often cross content disciplinary lines.

ACTIVITIES   As they encounter and analyze these projects, students investigate many facets of issues while they cope with finding valid research resources. As students make connections among ideas, they develop new skills and work on a variety of tasks, often in cooperative work groups. Students use the tools of the real world to complete their investigations, and often those tools include the wide variety of technology tools available—software applications, projection devices, the Internet, e-mail, and multimedia. As students investigate, they get feedback from coaches and experts about the validity of their ideas and sources.

CONDITIONS   Project-based learning underscores students' autonomy as they take part in inquiry and pursue solutions in a cooperative social context. Projects are lengthy and require students to develop and use time management skills, both individually and as part of a group. In taking on the tasks of researchers, reporters, planners, managers, and other roles, students direct their own work and take control of their own learning.

RESULTS   Project-based learning results in real-world outcomes as students create models, reports, multimedia presentations, skits, and other products that demonstrate what they have learned. Students are responsible for determining how they are going to demonstrate knowledge with peers, and the students themselves take part in assessing their projects. A project analysis sheet and class discussion can facilitate such assessment. As students engage in these activities, they often show growth in social skills and self-management, and a disposition for learning on their own—the skills promoted by the 1991 Secretary's Commission on Achieving Necessary Skills (SCANs) report. The full SCANs report can be found at **http://pueblo.pc.maricopa. edu/MariMUSE/SCANS/SCANS.html**.

An Example of Project-Based Learning

To introduce a project to students, the teacher would assign the group to be members of President Washington's cabinet after the Revolutionary War. Students would then be asked to advise the new president on how to bring the country together in setting up a new government. With a history of strong ties to the British, the new nation has citizens whose relatives still reside on the British Isles.

CONTENT   Students would research the causes and consequences of the Revolutionary War as well as information about the people who lived during that time. This would cross the curricular areas of social studies, economics, literature, and ethics and could require delving into the art and music.

ACTIVITIES   Students would gather and analyze information regarding the issues from texts, library books, and a wealth of information on the Internet from historical sites. Taking that information into account, students would hypothesize about various scenarios and then come up with advice for Washington.

CONDITIONS   Students engage in independent and group investigations of this post Revolutionary War scenario. They determine for themselves how they will fulfill the project requirements, noting that there is no "right" answer—only rigorous thinking—required in their end product. Students select and analyze their own resources, determining which are most valid. Work is collaborative with teams of students and with outside resources.

RESULTS   Students determine their own end product to demonstrate their learning. Such projects might be as varied as a debate, a multimedia report on the consequences of cutting off all ties with the British, a report on the discussion of personal rights, or a presentation on how the country might be if the British had won. Regardless of the end product, students will have shown that they can evaluate sources for historical accuracy or bias, that they can make decisions about which sources to use, and that they understand ambiguity in real-world problems.

Advantages of Project-Based Learning

The overall advantages of project-based learning are that students become responsible for their own learning and that their learning is presented in an authentic manner. Learning becomes relevant and personal to students as they become increasingly competent at searching for answers and solving real-world problems. Additionally, project-based learning allows information to be connected to students' prior knowledge as well as connected across curricula. It also promotes higher levels of cognitive processing.

Additionally, project-based learning supports meeting the individual student learning needs. Project-based learning can accommodate students' different intelligences and allows students to demonstrate their knowledge in ways that take advantage of those intelligences. Students' end products may highlight musical, artistic, technology, language, acting, or other skills. Collaborative and social skills are also promoted as students work in groups in noncompetitive settings.

Students become the owners of new knowledge as they defend their positions to their peers and others. Gaining knowledge through experience of making connections with prior experience in a social setting remains with students.

Finally, project-based learning and technology can build on each other as technology skills are used to solve real-world problems. For many students, this use of technology is intrinsically motivating and a good match with project-based learning. When students need to solve real-world problems, they need to do so with real-world tools. The Internet provides students access to resources, both print and human, as well as primary source documents. Students engaged in project-based learning activities have received responses from scientists, artists, and participants in historical events. Additionally, computing power allows students to deal with the huge amounts of data that must be analyzed across many projects. And finally, sophisticated presentation tools encourage students to create professional presentations to demonstrate their understanding.

Disadvantages of Project-Based Learning

Launching project-based learning for the first time can be a difficult transition for both students and teachers who are accustomed to a traditional approach. The change from essays, reports, multiple choice tests, and the like is akin to going thorough a cultural shift. It is difficult, especially for students who have learned how to get good grades on tests and papers. Creating projects requires quite different skill sets than the traditional means of assessment; it is not unlikely that such students will plead for a return to quizzes, tests, and the things "real teachers" do as they fear the unfamiliar territory of being responsible for creating the solution rather than being told there is only one way to be correct.

For teachers, it may be difficult to step aside and give students more control over their own learning, particularly because this does not mean less teacher preparation. The complexities of guiding students through tasks, constructing cooperative learning groups, and grading complex projects are both time-consuming and ambiguous. There is no crystal clear "right answer" found in a multiple-choice test.

Perhaps the most common criticism of project-based learning is that it sacrifices breadth for depth in covering materials. This is particularly problematic for districts that overly emphasize standardized test scores. Some of this concern can be ameliorated by carefully constructing projects that demonstrate meeting state and national standards, Nonetheless, higher test scores do not always follow, and the criticism stands.

It is also more difficult and time consuming to obtain evidence of a student's knowledge and understanding, particularly because grading must be done on many levels—such as language skills, technology skills, presentation skills, research skills, and group skills. Not only is assessment time-consuming, the time required for teachers to suggest or create projects can take many more hours than a lecture and multiple-choice test. Some of this time, but not all, can be recouped as students work independently on projects with teachers advising but not directing them. However, the preparation reflects the complexity of the projects themselves.

What Is Problem-Based Learning?

Problem-based learning is a curricular approach that develops problem-solving ability, interdisciplinary knowledge, and cross-curricular skills. Its first application was in medical schools where students solved real-world problems in diagnosis and treatment. In problem-based learning, students are confronted with a messy, ill-defined problem with insufficient information and the necessity to determine the best solution possible in a limited time. This structure develops problem-solving skills, a specific knowledge base, and inquiry skills. It is student-centered, as teachers give only guidelines for how to solve problems. Assessment, like project-based learning, is performance-based. Likewise, content, activities, conditions, and results are similar to project-based learning.

An Example of Problem-Based Learning

Problem-based learning is usually introduced with an "entry document" that defines the students' roles in a real-life problem. The entry document, which loosely defines the problem and the students' task, is written as a real-world document might be. In this case, a group of students will be given the role of consultants to the

CONTENT   Department of Fish and Game and asked to create a plan to reintroduce wolves to Yellowstone National Park.

Students research Yellowstone National Park, ranching on the park's boundaries, the views of those who live and work near the park, the environmental requirements for wolf packs, and the reasons the wolves are no longer in the area.

ACTIVITIES   Students may conduct research through national parks sites on the World Wide Web, by interviewing local national park rangers, interviewing national park employees by e-mail, talking to local ranchers or farmers about predation, as well as the numerous standard ways of doing research using libraries and texts. When students have done their research and come up with a plan, a new element is introduced to the problem.

This introduction of new information is a major facet of what distinguishes problem- from project-based learning. Students may, for example, be told that hearings on their wolf reintroduction plan resulted in overwhelming negative testimony. Students are apprised of the testimony (which may be engendered by other groups of students) and are then required to assess the criticisms as they come in, alter their hypotheses, and come up with a new solution to the plan to reintroduce wolves.

CONDITIONS   Students in this scenario need to analyze data for accuracy and make determinations about the validity and usefulness of the data. They need to deal with ambiguity as they reorganize and synthesize information. Students are given wide latitude on how to search for information, and the role of the teacher remains that of a guide—one of many experts or sources that may be accessed for information. As students work, they deal with multiple perspectives on the reintroduction scenario and learn to read and listen carefully, assessing multiple pieces of information.

PERFORMANCE   As in project-based learning, the end product of problem-based learning is a performance that synthesizes information and presents it to peers and the community. In this case, the product is the revised plan for reintroducing wolves to Yellowstone. The product is graded on the extent to which students took the complexity of the situation into account. It would also be graded for language skills, presentation skills, group work, technology skills, and research skills.

Advantages of Problem-Based Learning

Students who engaged in problem-based learning acquire multiple life skills. They must develop multiple hypotheses as they find, evaluate, and use data from multiple sources. They learn to deal with multiple perspectives and learn that in the real world, "right answers" are rare to nonexistent. Students must alter hypotheses as new information becomes available and must find solutions based on clear reasoning, using information that fits the problem. Additionally, they learn cooperative skills as they work in groups to solve these problems. They develop an appreciation for other points of view, and they develop the ability to defend their own points of view. As in project-based learning, the learning becomes their own.

Disadvantages of Problem-Based Learning

Problem-based learning carries with it the same disadvantages of project-based learning. Breadth is necessarily sacrificed for depth, it requires complex planning, and it is a cultural shift for both students and teachers. Additionally, it is more difficult to obtain evidence of students' knowledge.

Conclusion

Both project- and problem-based learning are based on students' active inquiry. By evaluating new ideas, relating cross-curricular concepts, and working cooperatively, students engage in higher-order thinking skills. Projects and problems usually are intrinsically interesting to students, leading them to use a variety of real-world tools and resources creatively to produce imaginative end products. Students become empowered to take charge of their own learning, and when that happens, much of the resistance to schooling evaporates. It is not uncommon for teachers to report students who come early to school, want to miss recess, stay late, and even ask that school be opened on weekends so that they can work on projects. Students become self-directed learners and carry the skills and attitudes they learn from project-based learning into other areas of their lives.

References

Material for this article was adapted from the following sources:

Aufdenspring, Deborah. "Project Based Learning: A Deliberate Design for Learning." Workshop for Montgomery Schools. Brewster Technology High School. Montgomery, Alabama. July 2000.

Buck Institute. "PBL Overview." *Project-based Learning.* **www.bie.org/pbl/overview/intro.html** (n.d.).

Illinois Mathematics and Science Academy. "Center for Problem Based Learning." *What is PBL?* **www.imsa.edu/team/cpbl/problem.html** (10 April 2001).

Maxwell, Nan L., Yolanda Bellisimo, John Mergendoller. "Problem Based Learning: Modifying the Medical School Model for Teaching High School Economics." *Proceedings of the American Educational Research Association* Session 3: 08 (1999).

Schools of California Online Resources for Education. "Problem Based Learning." *Internet Classrooms* **http://score.rims.k12.ca.us/problearn.html** (n.d.).

BY MIKE MENCHACA

Everything You Wanted to Know about Internet Filters

Almost everyone will agree that there are pictures, text, and other kinds of information on the Internet that is inappropriate for school-age children. Because it would be impossible for teachers to preview every Web site or continually look over each student's shoulder, most educators, parents, and others in the community believe that schools must set up some alternative ways of screening information before it reaches the student's computer monitor. This screening usually is done by one or more kinds of Internet filters.

What Are Filters?

The question about filters is a bit more complicated than one might think. As a concept, a filter is easy to understand. Basically, a filter is a mechanism that helps ensure children and young adults can't intentionally or accidentally access inappropriate information. Filters attempt to accomplish this task in many different ways. In fact, some of the best ways to filter information do not require technology at all!

In order to recognize the effect filters might have in your particular environment, it is important to understand the various forms filters take. While the information provided below does contain technical information, it also provides practical examples as a way of illustrating the various approaches to filtering. In most school districts, the initial filtering takes place long before the information reaches the classroom or lab computer. This filtering may be done at the school, district, or county office level.

It may not be important to remember all the techno-babble surrounding filters, but it is important to have a general sense of their purpose and how filtering is done in order to understand why you may or may not be able to access information. Having at least a general understanding of some of the technical requirements of filters will allow you to have more productive discussions with administrators and technical support personnel at your school site. An understanding of filters may help you make better decisions about what types of filters are needed at your site, and, more important, what types of filters are not needed.

ISTE ALERT!

The Federal Communications Commission released rules implementing the Children's Internet Protection Act (CIPA) in April 2001. CIPA mandates that schools and libraries receiving E-Rate discounts and certain other federal technology funding, put into place

Internet safety policies that include installation and use of Internet filtering software beginning July 1, 2001.

The filtering measures are intended to prevent access to "visual depictions" of material that is obscene, that depicts child pornography, and—when minors are using the computer—that is considered to be harmful to minors. These rules only apply to those schools and libraries receiving E-Rate discounts.

For more information, visit the FCC Web site at **www.fcc.gov.**

What Types of Filtering Should I Know About?

Technically speaking, filtering refers to the ability of an intermediating agency to control the type and flow of information from one location to another. Practically speaking, filtering refers to the task of screening information to prevent inappropriate information from reaching your students. More and more often, filtering is done by technical support personnel at some location removed from the classroom, such as a district office, a county office, or even by on-site staff. In these instances, filtering is usually controlled through the use of software on a proxy server, that is, a computer that can look at information to determine what is and what is not appropriate. While there are many methods for filtering information, the proxy server method is one of the most popular. The concept of a proxy server is fairly simple to understand.

After you have finished reading this chapter, you should have a better understanding of filtering methods in general and proxy servers in specific and how the flow of information can be regulated in school settings.

What Is a Proxy Server?

In voting, a proxy is someone or some group that you empower with the ability to cast a vote in your place. For example, you may fill out and send in a proxy authorization card to a retirement fund in which you participate. This proxy authorization might allow a specific manager or board to vote for you on matters related to the management of the retirement fund. You are entrusting your vote and assuming that the manager or board will understand your best interests. This is a very common procedure in areas that might not be your expertise. In the particular example given, you might not understand how best to manage and operate a retirement fund to ensure that it builds maximum value over time. You are empowering an individual or group of individuals you believe to have such expertise to use your vote wisely.

A proxy server works much in the same way. Although you might be sitting at a specific computer in a classroom or laboratory, all the information that you send to or request from the World Wide Web actually passes through another computer, the proxy server. As far as the Web is concerned, the information coming from your location all comes from and then goes to a single computer, even if that information originated from computers all over your campus. In essence, the proxy computer is serving as your designated proxy, and, just as in our voting example, it decides what your best interest is. If the proxy server determines that certain information is inappropriate, then it refuses to forward the information to your computer for display. Similarly, if the proxy server determines that you are trying to send out information that is inappropriate, it forbids that information from ever leaving your site. Every bit of information that you request from or send out to the Internet must first pass through and be approved by the proxy server. How does the proxy server determine what is or is not appropriate? It uses filtering software.

In addition to providing filtering, a proxy server also caches information that is frequently accessed and approved. For example, imagine a computer lab setting in which students at 32 lab workstations are required to access the White House home page to complete a class assignment. To speed access, a proxy server learns that the White House home page is frequently visited by these workstations, and instead of having to traverse the Internet each time to download the Web site, a proxy server temporarily downloads the information and displays the Web site directly to the workstations itself. In short, the proxy server caches frequently visited home pages and then sends them directly to connected workstations much more quickly than if these workstations had to download the information directly from the Internet each and every time.

The benefits of proxy servers include the ability to protect users and children from discovering and viewing inappropriate information. In addition, caching capabilities of proxy server significantly increase the speed of access to information on the Internet.

The drawbacks of proxy servers can include situations in which legitimate information is prevented from being displayed. In addition, because workstations have to first request information from the proxy server and cannot themselves go directly to other computers on the Internet, during busy-time periods a proxy server can actually slow down access to information on the Internet. This occurs at times when many computers (especially in a lab setting) are requesting information from the Internet through the proxy server at the same time.

What Is Filtering Software?

Filtering software can be installed on proxy servers, on other servers, or on a single computer to accomplish many different goals. Indeed, there are many methods by which filtering software accomplishes the task of analyzing and approving information to be displayed. These methods use different ways that computers communicate on the Internet to help filter out information.

In addition to proxy servers, other forms of filtering include Web portals, kid-safe search engines, supervision, specialized applications, and common sense. These methods will be discussed following the section on proxy servers.

ADDRESS SUPPRESSION

One method of filtering information is called TCP/IP address suppression or IP packet filtering. In this method, a proxy server looks at the Internet address of each piece (or packet) of information that is trying to pass through the server to determine whether a particular address might be "blacklisted." That is, the proxy server looks at incoming information, determines from where that information is coming, and checks its database of addresses to see whether the information originated from a location that has been flagged as containing inappropriate information.

The benefit to this method is that proxy servers can determine quickly that entire sites contain inappropriate information and prevent that information from being displayed. Another benefit is that this method gives technical support staff the opportunity to determine which sites on the Internet should be displayed and which should be suppressed from view.

The drawback to this method is that the technical support staff must continually update the list of restricted addresses that the proxy server will block. If the list of addresses is not continually updated, it is possible that students may visit inappropriate sites. In addition, because entire sites are suppressed, the situation might occur in which some legitimate and important information from one of these sites is blocked.

KEYWORD SUPPRESSION

Another method for filtering information is called keyword suppression. In this method, the filtering software on the proxy server checks all text passing through to determine whether there might be "inappropriate" words in the text. The proxy server contains a list of words deemed inappropriate, and if any of these words appear in information headed for its network, the server prevents that information from continuing forward.

The benefit to this method is that Web pages, e-mail messages, or documents containing certain keywords can easily be prevented from being displayed. It is a simple matter to construct a list of words or phrases that are considered inappropriate.

The drawback to this method is that the proxy server can actually suppress sites that are desired and appropriate. For example, certain pages on sex education might be inappropriate for children in the primary grades. However, such information might be needed for sex education classes at higher grade levels. If the proxy server prevents all pages with certain words from being displayed, even those that might appropriately come up in a sex education situation will be suppressed. It should be noted, however, that in most cases the technical support staff can "approve" certain Web sites even when they contain keywords that normally are suppressed.

APPLICATION OR PROTOCOL FILTERING

A final method for filtering information is called application filtering (also called port or protocol filtering). In this method, a proxy server keeps certain kinds of applications (or protocols) from passing any information either to the Internet or its own users. An example of this kind of filtering is the blocking of chat rooms. Chat rooms use a certain kind of protocol, or method, for communicating. A proxy server recognizes when users are trying to chat and can simply not allow this to happen on its network. Other kinds of applications or protocols proxy servers frequently block include FTP (or the transfer of files such as games), electronic mail, and telnet (logging on to other computers).

The benefits of protocol filtering include the ability to prevent individuals from engaging in activities deemed inappropriate, such as chatting or downloading files (usually games). In addition, because most proxy servers filter information only on actual Web pages, some inappropriate material might be transferred through chat rooms or FTP sites if protocol filtering isn't used.

The drawbacks to protocol filtering include situations in which access to filtered applications is necessary. For example, application filtering might prevent staff development training activities from taking place in a lab when participants need to download files, upload Web pages, or even chat with teachers across the country with similar interests. In addition, situations might arise in which students have the opportunity to chat with experts in the field—mathematicians, scientists, politicians, sports figures, musicians—or download shareware and freeware applications. Protocol filtering would prevent some of these legitimate uses.

A valuable resource for finding Internet filtering software that meets your specific needs can be found at **www.getnetwise.org/tools.** They list more than 140 Internet filtering software programs and allow a search based on specific criteria you request.

Other Methods for Controlling Access to Internet Information

Methods for filtering information using proxy servers may be overly controlling, prevent the transfer of legitimate information, or miss information that is inappropriate in a particular classroom setting. There are many other methods for controlling the flow of information. Such methods include Web portals, kid-safe search engines, supervision, applications for downloading information to be presented later or in a classroom without Internet access, and, of course, common sense.

While the following descriptions do not attempt to cover all methods for filtering information, they do provide a basis for understanding and approaching the complex task of controlling the flow of information, especially to young children.

EDUCATIONAL WEB PORTALS

Educational Web portals are Web sites that act as clearinghouses for information, lesson plans, and other resources. They may even provide e-mail, chat rooms, and discussion lists related to technology affecting the classroom. A Web portal attempts to be comprehensive and uses a "one-stop shopping" approach. That is, a Web portal hopes to contain all the information a visitor will ever need on a specific subject. With such a comprehensive approach, designers of Web portals hope to capture the attention of Internet users so that they are less tempted to look for information elsewhere. Web portals benefit from this by providing links to vendors, advertising banners, or charging a small monthly fee to generate income.

There are many excellent educational Web portals for students and teacherson the World Wide Web. Some examples include Classroom Connect, Ed's Oasis, the Teaching Portal, and Education World (see Table 1 for URLs). The excellent education Web portals have real people evaluating the resources before they add links to the Web pages. Other portals have software "bots" that search the Web for resources that meet certain criteria. These sites may well have links to sites that teachers may find to be inappropriate for their students for a variety of reasons.

Some benefits of educational Web portals include many resources in matters related to education; communications-based technologies that allow teachers, students, parents, and administrators to interact with each other; and a means by which educators can improve their own practice.

Some drawbacks to Web portals include that the sites must process much Web-based information to determine what is and what is not useful. Because humans process information much more slowly than computers do, Web portals might not necessarily contain the latest resources available. In addition, the Web portal makes the decision as to what is and what is not appropriate. Web portals must determine which resources are most significant, and others might not always agree with those decisions.

TABLE 1   **Education Resource Portals**

FOR TEACHERS	FOR CHILDREN
Classroom Connect **www.classroom.com**	Discovery Kids **http://kids.discovery.com**
Ed's Oasis **www.classroom.com/edsoasis**	DiscoverySchool.com **http://school.discovery.com/kids**
Education World **www.education-world.com**	Kids Domain **www.kidsdomain.com**
Teachers First **http://school.discovery.com/schrockguide**	Kidscom **www.kidscom.com**
Teaching Portal **www.teachingportal.com**	

KID-SAFE SEARCH ENGINES

Another type of filtering involves providing students with search engines that are known to be safe. That is, similar to Web portals, an agency analyzes information to determine whether it is appropriate to be shared with students at various ages.

The benefit of kid-safe search engines is that teachers, parents, and administrators can be certain that information found on the site will be appropriate for children. This can be a tremendous time saver for assignments that require students to find resources on the Internet.

The drawback to kid-safe search engines is that, just as with Web portals, an agency can process information only so fast and newer resources added might not be available. Similarly, most search engines make determinations about the appropriateness of information but not necessarily about the educational utility of that same information. That is, a kid-safe search engine might determine that a site is safe, but that does not ensure that the information is educationally sound. For more information on the types of kid-safe search engines available, please see the following chapter on search engines.

SUPERVISION

Although many different methods exist to ensure that information is appropriate, there is still not an adequate substitute for adult supervision. For all the cyber-nanny and Web-babysitter sites that exist, adult supervision is still critical.

Students must be taught how to evaluate and determine the appropriateness, accuracy, and benefit of information found online. Anyone can put up a Web page on any subject. Therefore, the accuracy of information on Web pages should be independently determined either by (a) assuring that the information came from a reliable source, (b) comparing it with other sites with similar information, or (c) consulting an adult or teacher about the information.

In addition, even when information is determined to be accurate, it still may not have educational value. Teachers still play a critical role in ensuring that students have access to the best and most appropriate information to be found on the Internet.

COMMON SENSE

Finally, common sense while using the Internet is critical. Leaving students unattended in a situation where no filtering is available certainly is not advised. However, providing too many restrictions can also be problematic. Using your own best judgment when dealing with Web-based information is important and should not be undervalued.

Conclusion

Obviously, filtering and technologies associated with filtering are more complicated issues than first meet the eye. However, understanding some basic concepts and approaches to filtering will better allow you to implement filtering techniques at your own site.

Table 2 on the next page is provided as a synopsis of the information contained in this chapter. With this information, you are one step closer to understanding some of the complexities associated with Internet usage.

TABLE 2   **Types of Filtering and Synopses of Their Pros and Cons**

TYPES OF FILTERING	PROS	CONS
Proxy Servers	Provide protection from inappropriate material; speed access by *caching* (remembering) Web pages	Can filter out appropriate material; can slow down access to the Internet during peak periods
Address Suppression Software	Can identify entire sites deemed inappropriate; gives technical staff control over the flow of information	Must be continually updated to handle new sites; would suppress legitimate information needed from a banned site
Keyword Suppression Software	Can quickly distinguish inappropriate information by searching for banned words; searches many types of computerized material containing text	Might ban words appropriate in specific cases; can slow down access to the Internet
Application or Protocol Filtering Software	Can easily block chat, file downloading, e-mail, and telnet	Would prevent users with legitimate reasons from chatting, downloading files, communicating by e-mail, or logging on to libraries with telnet
Educational Web Portals	Provide access to educational resources; organize resources that are easy to find; allow communication with other students and educators	Must keep up with constant updates to and new additions of critical resources; might charge a fee for service; might contain commercial advertisements
Kid-Safe Search Engines	Provide access to preapproved resources; organize resources so kids can find them easily	Can only include resources actually evaluated; do not guarantee the educational reliability of the resources
Supervision	Ensures students do not view inappropriate material	Requires an investment of human resources

chapter
4

BY MIKE MENCHACA

Search Engines Explained

Methods for indexing and retrieving information have existed almost since the moment humankind started keeping records. When Ptolemy I established the great Library of Alexandria in 290 B.C., he also created a way to store and retrieve its important documents. In the latter half of the 19th century, Melvil Dewey invented a classification system with a standard index to search and retrieve books and documents.

The Internet and the World Wide Web contain a wealth of documents, journals, articles, books, and more. However, all this information is useless unless there is a way to locate the documents you need. As a result of the popularity of the World Wide Web as a source for information, many organizations and companies have created incredibly fast and complex databases to help users search and locate specific items from its wealth of information. These companies and organizations have taken several different approaches to collecting, indexing, and then searching through the information.

This chapter should help you understand how search engines collect information, how to search through the information that is collected, and finally, how to find specialized collections and engines appropriate for children and young adults.

How Do Search Engines Collect Information?

Search engines use several methods for collecting and indexing information from the World Wide Web. Two methods are the most common:

- Using spiders and bots, which rely heavily on technology.
- Compiling and categorizing information, which requires significant human resources.

SPIDERS AND BOTS

A popular method for collecting information from the Web uses spiders, or Web crawlers, which navigate through the Web on their own, following links and fetching information, which is added to a huge, powerful existing database (example, AltaVista). These spiders are automated robots—hence, the term "bots"—that require intense and powerful computer processors and massive amounts of storage space.

The benefit of using spiders and bots to gather information is that the information can be gathered and made available quickly and easily. The spiders and bots allow for a very large amount of information to be collected and indexed.

The drawback to this method of collecting information is that spiders and bots make no determination as to the appropriateness of material collected and often index inappropriate or useless information.

COMPILED AND
CATEGORIZED
INFORMATION

Another popular method for collecting information requires humans to actually review, approve, and categorize material (example, Yahoo!). This method uses human resources to organize Web-based information into categories that can then be searched in much the same manner as the Dewey Decimal System.

For example, a university might ask the owners of a search engine to include the university Web page on the search site. As soon as the search site receives such a request, someone will review the site, approve it, and then determine the category or categories in which it should be placed. In this particular example, the search site might determine the university's Web site should be placed in several categories including the state within which the university is located, its status as a private or public institution, its areas of specialty such as liberal arts or technology, and the graduate degrees it offers, if any.

The benefit to this method of gathering information is that some set of rules guides the indexing process. A human or group of humans actually reviews the information to determine its most-likely categorization and whether the information appears to be legitimate.

The drawback to this method is that it can be very slow and labor intensive. Humans process information much more slowly than computers, and time limits mean that many Web pages containing potentially useful information are not indexed. In addition, with this method, content is categorized but not necessarily processed for appropriateness or educational soundness. That is, a site might be appropriately called kid-friendly, but not necessarily analyzed to determine whether it has any educational value.

Once Information Is Collected

What methods exist for searching information once it is collected and indexed? Some basic approaches to Web search engines include keyword search engines, natural language search engines, subject guides, and metasearch engines. These groupings are not the only way to categorize search engines, but they do offer a convenient approach to better understand search engines and search strategies.

KEYWORD SEARCH
ENGINES

Keyword search engines allow users to enter key terms that are then checked against large, powerful databases that were created and added to by spiders and bots. Based on the keywords entered, the engine retrieves matching information and displays it in some prescribed order. Keyword search engines range from very simple ones to ones that utilize complex search strategies such as Boolean logic (visit AltaVista at **www.av.com** for a comprehensive explanation of Boolean logic).

Keyword search engines are most useful for finding specific pieces of information, especially those with uncommon words or specific phrases or titles. For example, it is much easier to find the phrase "War and Peace" than it is to find all those documents that contain both the word "war" and the word "peace" in them. Keyword search engines are less effective in finding general subjects or categories.

<table>
<tr><td>**ISTE TIP**</td><td>*Remove search engine frames to get Web addresses. Search engines often leave the site you searched for within a frame of their site. This does not allow you to see your site's actual Web address easily. Click the Remove Frames button provided (usually at the top of the window) and you will remove the frame and see only the site you requested and its URL.*</td></tr>
</table>

The benefit to using keyword search engines is that searches can often be done quickly and easily, especially for finding titles, phrases, or uncommon words. In addition, the use of Boolean logic can help control how you approach looking for information (finding related words or excluding words) as well as how the information is then organized (level of confidence, number of times a keyword is found).

The drawbacks to keyword search engines include too many false hits (documents that do not really contain what you are seeking), too many documents to search through, and too many documents that are unrelated or only marginally related. In addition, while Boolean logic can be very helpful, constructing appropriate searches can take time, patience, and understanding.

TABLE 3 **Examples of Keyword Search Engines**

FOR ADULTS	FOR CHILDREN
AltaVista: www.altavista.com	AOL: www.aol.com/netfind/kids/
Excite: www.excite.com	Cyber Patrol's CyberGuide: www.route616.com
Infoseek: www.infoseek.com	Quality Search Engine: www.a1source.com/
Lycos: www.lycos.com	Saluki Search: www.salukisearch.com
Webcrawler: www.Webcrawler.com	

Natural Language Search Engines

Natural language engines allow you to perform searches by entering phrases or complete sentences, rather than using just keywords or Boolean logic. The natural language search engine will dissect your sentence or phrase and create search criteria based on syntax, structure, words, and so forth. This method is especially useful for younger kids who might not yet be adequately skilled at methods of applying logic to solve a problem.

The benefits of natural language search engines include the speed of searching and not having to develop a complex search strategy.

One drawback is that complex searches can't be done easily with a natural language search engine. Logic and meaning can be misinterpreted or too many variables might be present in these searches.

TABLE 4 **Natural Language Search Engines**

FOR ADULTS	FOR CHILDREN
Ask Jeeves: **www.askjeeves.com**	Ask Jeeves: **www.ajkids.com**

Subject Guides

Subject guides organize information and Web sites by categories. Searchers can then browse certain categories or subjects, much like a using a card catalog, to find the subject closest to what they are seeking. As mentioned previously, subject guides are organized by humans who have applied some set of criteria in making the selections.

One benefit of subject guides is that the information fetched is generally what you expect it to be. That is, if you are looking at the subject "cars," the information contained within that category will be related to cars and not sites that just happened to mention the words cars within them. In addition, subject guides tend not to present a glut of Web sites that need further refinement and perusal.

One drawback to subject guides is that information is not necessarily evaluated, only categorized. In addition, it is difficult to find specific pieces of information or documents, especially as related to research. Another drawback is that subject guides categorize and index information and Web sites mostly by their major components. In some cases, information can be there but not indexed because it wasn't located on the site's main page.

TABLE 5 **Subject Guide Search Engines**

FOR ADULTS	FOR CHILDREN
LookSmart: **www.looksmart.com** Magellan: **http://magellan.excite.com** Yahoo: **www.yahoo.com**	KidsClick!: **http://sunsite.berkeley.edu/KidsClick!/** Yahooligans: **www.yahooligans.com**

Metasearch Engines

The final type of search engine discussed here allows you to search several other search engines at the same time. For example, a group of Stanford students started the search engine Google because they felt that most search engines had too much extraneous material. Google has an uncluttered, streamlined interface and, in addition to having its own search capability, can simultaneously search for information on engines such as Yahoo!, Lycos, and AltaVista. Other metaengines, such as Dogpile, do not have their own search capabilities but instead allow users to search information found by other search engines.

The benefit of metasearch engines is the ability to quickly look for information located by many different search engines at the same time. Often, information can be found quickly and easily. Some metasearch engines also allow you to specify the type of information you are trying to locate, such as multimedia files, audio files, and discussion list archives.

One drawback to metasearch engines is that users have less control over the format of their search terms. For example, metasearches might allow you to search AltaVista but will not allow you to enter your search terms using Boolean logic.

TABLE 6 **Metasearch Engines**

FOR ADULTS	FOR CHILDREN
Dogpile: www.dogpile.com Google: www.google.com HotBot: www.hotbot.com	Family Friendly Search: **www.familyfriendlysearch.com/**

Summary

As you can see, there are many different types of search engines and approaches to finding information on the Internet and Web. As with any form of research, there is no one right approach. Experienced researchers do not expect to peruse only a library's card catalog or a single online index to find all of the information needed. Just as library-based requires an exhaustive search strategy, so do online researchers need to look at indexes, catalogs, CD-ROMs, microfiche, and many other formats to find information.

Similarly, your approach to finding information online should be conducted the same way. Use all of the available resources and search engines at your disposal. Keep in mind that no one search engine will be able to meet all of your needs. This should also help with frustration when you are having difficulty finding information. If you have tried a specific search engine for a half-hour or more and still cannot find pertinent information, try another search engine!

SEARCH ENGINE STRATEGIES

The table on the next page indicates some of the ways to approach using search engines. This table by no means should be misconstrued as the only or even the best method for approaching searches. It is merely given as an example of how conducting searches in certain instances might be accomplished. As you conduct searches, keep track of which search engines are your favorites and for what reasons. Eventually, you will develop your own search style.

FOR MORE INFORMATION

For more information on search engines, link to the University of South Carolina, Beaufort Library tutorial on search engines and search engine strategies: **www.sc.edu/beaufort/library/bones.html**.

TABLE 7   **Approaches to Conducting Web-Based Searches**

WHAT YOU KNOW	MOST APPROPRIATE SEARCH ENGINES
A specific company or organization	Subject guides or metasearch engines
An author, famous person, or historical figure	Subject guides or natural language search engines
A title or phrase	Keyword or metasearch engines
A general question	Natural language search engines
Specific question	Boolean logic, keyword search engines
Complex information	Boolean logic, keyword search engines
A specific kind of document (multimedia, audio file, etc.)	Search engines that allow you to search by format (Dogpile, Yahoo!, etc.)

chapter 5

BY WALTER MCKENZIE

Constructing a Rubric

As constructivist instructional practices have become part of the mainstream in education, assessment rubrics have gained in popularity. Teachers no longer teach the curriculum or teach the text; they teach the child. Their role is not to disseminate information but to support learners in building understandings. The rubric is an excellent tool for assessing student progress in this type of educational environment. It frees teachers from the limitations of traditional pencil and paper assessments and places the focus on student performance.

It sounds wonderful, but how does a teacher go about creating a rubric that will successfully measure student learning? There is a deliberate set of steps in designing an original rubric:

- State the lesson objective.
- Design an assessment task that allows the student to demonstrate his or her success in mastering the objective.
- Develop a set of observable, measurable criteria that can be used to measure the assessment task.
- Identify levels or degrees of success for the criteria.
- Craft statements that describe each level of success for each criterion.

Let's take a closer look at each step of the process.

State the Lesson Objective

As in any effective lesson, the instructional objective must be stated up front. It is the foundation on which the entire lesson is built, including the assessment. The objective should be stated in concrete terms clearly identifying the task the learner will be asked to accomplish. Teachers are trained in the writing of objectives, and this becomes second nature as they gain experience in the classroom.

However, the challenge of the objective may not be in how it is stated, but how it is crafted. If teachers simply state that given pencil and paper the student will complete an objective test on Greek and Roman forms of government with at least 70% accuracy, they will get exactly what they have asked for: rote recall of facts and figures to successfully fill in blanks. It's quick and it's easily measured, but does it really give an accurate idea of what students have learned? On the other hand, consider the ways students would demonstrate their understanding of early Western forms of government if the objective asked them to create a Venn diagram showing the similarities and differences between the Greek and Roman systems. Now students have to apply their knowledge to compare and contrast both systems of government.

Faced with the choice of these two assessment tasks, teachers have traditionally stuck with the objective test because there were not a lot of options available for accurately measuring student learning if there was more than one right answer. What if different students use different idioms for expressing their understanding? Doesn't it become hard to manage if there is no finite set of acceptable responses to the assessment task? And how do teachers quantify degrees of success when every student's Venn diagram can be so unique? The rubric can address all these questions. Most important, though, it invites teachers to craft assessment tasks that aren't looking for a single right answer. It allows students to perform at higher levels of thinking. The key is crafting assessment tasks that go beyond the objective to more open-ended, subjective activities.

Design an Assessment Task

Once you are satisfied you have an objective that allows for varied forms of student performance, you must craft an assessment task that will follow through on the intent of your objective. The single most common error teachers make in designing assessments is to create tasks that are not consistent with the lesson objective. For example, if students are to learn how to read the periodic table of the elements, it would be inconsistent to assess their understanding by asking each student to create their own imaginary element, all presented in a colorful drawing. It would make a creative bulletin board display for back to school night, but it would not measure the intended objective of the lesson: to accurately interpret the properties of the elements on the periodic table.

Rather, revisit the assessment task for measuring how accurately students can read and interpret the nomenclature on the periodic table by tweaking this creative idea. Yes, students can create original elements, but have them present their new discoveries by creating actual entries for the periodic table complete with symbols, atomic numbers, and all the details that make the table so useful. To extend the task, students could write a paragraph description of their new element, including how it was discovered, where it belongs on the periodic table, and what traits make it a new and unique element. In this way students can be imaginative while still being held to the standards set in the periodic table. If they can read and interpret one another's entries for new elements on the table, then they surely have mastered the prescribed skill in the objective.

Develop a Set of Observable, Measurable Criteria

With the objective and assessment task in place, the teacher is now ready to develop a list of criteria for assessing each student's work product. These criteria should be general enough to apply to a range of student products but specific enough that everyone can agree on their meaning. For the assessment task of creating and presenting an original element in the format of the periodic table, criteria might include:

- creation of an original symbol;

- indication of atomic number;

- inclusion of atomic weight;

- proper placement on the periodic table based on the element's characteristics; and

- a descriptive paragraph of at least five complete sentences that explains the origin and properties of this newfound element.

In addition, teachers may want to include other criteria on which they place emphasis in their classrooms:

- turned in on time

- neat and clean appearance

- free of errors

- proper heading included

This is the beauty of rubric construction. You decide which values to emphasize in evaluating student work.

For each of these examples, the criterion is succinctly stated, observable, and measurable in student work. Writing a concise set of criteria will take some soul-searching as you decide what you truly want to stress in assessing student work. But once you realize your priorities for learning, you will find the process highly rewarding for both yourself and your students.

Identify Degrees of Success for the Criteria

With your criteria in place, you are now ready to determine the degrees of success you want to establish for student work. A three-point rubric is always popular because it provides for basic levels of success: unsatisfactory, satisfactory, and exemplary. Then again, a four-point scale gives your rubric a greater sensitivity to degrees of student success: unsatisfactory, satisfactory, exemplary, and exceptional. The more levels you build in, the more sophisticated your rubric will be. If you want a quick and easy assessment tool, a three-point scale may suffice. Then again, if you're assessing major projects at the end of a unit, you may choose to develop a five-point scale that provides finer distinctions among degrees of success.

EXAMPLE RUBRIC **Periodic Table Rubric**

CRITERIA	1 UNSATISFACTORY	2 SATISFACTORY	3 EXEMPLARY
Creation of an original symbol			
Indication of atomic number			
Inclusion of atomic weight			
Proper placement on the periodic table based on the element's characteristics			
A descriptive paragraph of at least five complete sentences that explains the origin and properties of this newfound element			

For the periodic table rubric, I will select a three-point scale. I don't want to go into great detail because it is not a summative assessment. It would look like this:

With the criteria and levels of success in place, we are ready for the final step in creating our rubric.

Craft Exemplars for Each Criterion

What truly makes the rubric an effective assessment tool are the exemplars, or descriptors of success, for each criterion. In the table above the rubric is still incomplete. Anyone can arbitrarily assign points to a student work product based on their own subjective values. To make the rubric a truly objective instrument,

EXAMPLE RUBRIC EXCERPT **Periodic Table Rubric**

CRITERIA	1 UNSATISFACTORY	2 SATISFACTORY	3 EXEMPLARY
Creation of an original symbol	No symbol is evident or the symbol offered does not follow the conventions of the periodic table.	A symbol is offered that is consistent with the conventions of the periodic table.	A symbol is offered that is consistent with the conventions of the periodic table and reveals personality traits unique to this student.

exemplars are a must. Exemplars descriptively state the degrees of success for each criterion that both teacher and students can understand. Consider criterion 1, for example:

Exemplars are critical in filling out a rubric that offers meaningful feedback to students and parents. Once you have a rubric in place, you may choose to share it with your students before they begin their assessment task so that they will know the standards they are working to meet and exceed. In this way it becomes more than just another assessment tool. Your rubric actually becomes a key component in your instruction.

After teachers have modeled several rubrics themselves in the course of the school year, they may choose to engage their students in a discussion of what criteria should be included in assessing student work, actually building rubrics together. This takes constructivist teaching to an entirely new height, where students share in the responsibility for developing assessments and thereby take a greater ownership in their own learning. Moreover, actively involving students in rubric construction helps instill in them the high standards they need to set for themselves. Properly constructed rubrics can make all this happen for you in your classroom.

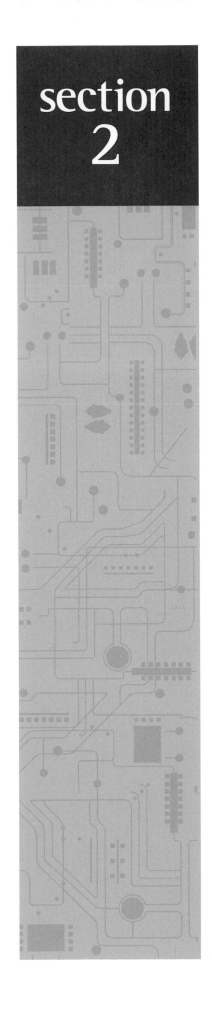

section 2

Resource Units

theme 1

BY MITCH HALL AND LINDA PERRY

" 'Think simple' as my old master used to say—meaning reduce the whole of its parts into the simplest terms, getting back to first principles."

—Frank Lloyd Wright

Form and Structure

The concept of form and structure can be applied in all areas of the curriculum as students study the way things are put together, from words and phrases to bridges and artwork. Because children need to see the big picture before breaking a topic down into its components, this theme immerses students in a variety of activities that help them make connections between broad, familiar experiences and new content-specific skills. By recognizing the patterns that permeate each of the units herein, students can make generalizations and form understandings that they can apply in a variety of contexts.

Form and structure is a topic ripe for technology because so many productivity applications require a recognition of building block elements and the patterns they create in communicating content and celebrating learning. Drawing software has its palettes, word processing has its toolbars, spreadsheets have formatting tools and formulae, databases have queries and filters, and the list goes on. Through this theme, then, students will not only investigate the form and structure of different kinds of technology, they will be empowered to employ it for rich, meaningful forms of expression.

The standards-based lessons in the following curriculum enable students to explore the concepts of form and structure as they

- investigate the literature patterns of international fairy tales;
- compose their own dance steps to demonstrate examples of rhythmic patterns;
- connect cultures and geometric designs in fabrics by studying quilts;
- blend concepts of geometry and art in an examination of tessellations;
- compose their own musical pieces to provide examples and show understanding of rhythmic "counting";
- build model kites, bridges, or castles to understand structural patterns;
- categorize and compare word configurations to examine language patterns;

and much, much more!

Unit Tools

Spreadsheets: Spreadsheets are integrated into the curriculum as students record data in an organized format. Charts are generated and results are compared.

Databases: Databases are used to categorize, sort and report data in meaningful ways so that students can use data to compare and predict.

Word Processing: Word processing is used for desktop publishing, text formatting, and support in each step of the writing process.

Drawing Software: Drawing software is used to create original digital images and manipulate shapes, lines and colors.

Digital Cameras and Video Cameras: Digital cameras and video cameras are used to capture pictures of student work as they complete group projects.

Multimedia Applications: Multimedia applications such as HyperStudio or PowerPoint are used to present student work by importing text, data, images and sound into a class presentation.

Web Browser: Students use Web sites to view slideshows and interact with tessellation properties, and even search for common misspellings online.

CHILDREN'S LITERATURE

The Big Wave by Pearl S. Buck
Cindrillon: A Caribbean Cinderella by San Souci
Eight Hands Round by Ann Paul
The Keeping Quilt by Patricia Polacco
Kente Colors by Deborah M. Newton Chocolate
Kofi and His Magic by Maya Angelou
Jambo Means Hello by Muriel Feelings
The Log Cabin Quilt by Ellen Howard
Moja Means One by Muriel Feelings
The Spider Weaver: A Legend of Kente Cloth by Margaret Musgrove
Hailstones and Halibut Bones by Mary O'Neil
Rainbow Crow by Nancy Van Laan
The Tenth Good Thing About Barney by Judith Viorst
With Needle and Thread: A Book About Quilts by Raymond Bial

WRITING ACROSS THE CURRICULUM

Many opportunities exist for students to practice their writing skills in this unit. They will have the opportunity to write poetry, fairy tales, tongue twisters, and nonsense words. In addition, they might wish to add descriptions of the cultural significance for their choice of colors to their work with fabric patterns. They could also describe in writing (either in script format to accompany a movie or in text format on a multimedia presentation) the structure or pattern to their music or dance creation. When contacting an expert to clear up confusion or seek advice while building a model, they will be practicing their written communication skills.

TEACHER VOICES

About the Language and Literature Unit

"Many students come to school having heard just one version of Cinderella. They will be surprised to discover that children from other countries have heard similar tales as they were growing up. In these units, children will analyze their language, from the smallest unit of sounds within words (spelling patterns), to the level of sounds combined in sentences (tongue twisters), all the way to the comparison of cultural variations in literature (fairy tales). They will be exposed to other languages and other lifestyles and compare them to their own."

About the Fabric Patterns and Tessellation Patterns Units

"Children are excited by their ability to create authentic-looking designs using computer drawing programs. What would be very difficult to create using a pencil and paper is quite easy to accomplish using drawing tools on the computer. Through access to images on the Internet or in books, the students gain an understanding of geometric patterns and the cultural significance of color choices for their designs. These units blend concepts of geometry, art, and culture as students produce appealing works of art."

WEB RESOURCES

Ask an Expert
  Pitsco's Ask an Expert: www.askanexpert.com
  CIESE Ask an Expert Sites: njnie.dl.stevens-tech.edu/askanexpert.html
  Focus Educational Services: www.studentsonly.net
  Kids Connect: www.ala.org/ICONN/AskKC.html
  LookSmart Ask an Expert for Students:
    www.looksmart.com/eus1/eus53706/eus53720/eus53813/eus150946/r?l&
  WonderKorner: www.peak.org/~bonwritr/wonder1.htm

Dance
  African Music and Dance Ensemble:
    www.cnmat.berkeley.edu/~ladzekpo/Ensemble.html
  Early Break Dancing: www.americaslibrary.gov/pages/jp_dance_break_1.html
  ThinkQuest Journey to New Worlds, Hula:
    tqjunior.thinkquest.org/6073/hawnres/hrhula.html
  Let's Dance Latin Style!: library.thinkquest.org/J002194F/
  The Shanghai Acrobatic Troupe: www.shanghaiacrobats.com

Fairy Tales
  Aesop's Fables—Traditional and Modern: www.umass.edu/aesop
  The Grimm Brothers: www.nationalgeographic.com/grimm/
  Myths, Folk Tales and Fairy Tales:
    teacher.scholastic.com/writewit/mff/fairytales_home.htm
  Absolutely Whootie—Stories to Grow By: www.storiestogrowby.com
  SurLaLune Fairy Tale Pages: members.aol.com/surlalune/frytales/index.htm

Models
  Ask ERIC, Building Bridges: http://askeric.org/cgi-bin/printlessons.cgi/
    Virtual/Lessons/Arts/Architecture/ARC0200.html
  Build It and Bust It: library.thinkquest.org/11686/
  Creative Classroom Online:
    www.creativeclassroom.org/mj00hotstuff/index2.html
  Look, Learn and Do: www.looklearnanddo.com/documents/home.html

Music
  CBC 4 Kids—Music: www.cbc4kids.ca/general/music/
  Music Genre Sampler: datadragon.com/education/genres/
  STOMP—Percussion for Kids: www.stomponline.com/percuss1.html

Turntables: www.turntables.de/start.htm#

Online Art Galleries

Art on the Net: www.art.net/

Eschart and Illusions: www.domaindlx.com/Escher/

The Museum of Modern Art, New York: moma.org/

Tessellating Animation: www18.big.or.jp/~mnaka/home.index.html

Webmuseum, Paris: www.ibiblio.org/wm/

Poetry

Crazy Limerick Machine:
www.ambleside.schoolzone.co.uk/ambleweb/year4/limerick.htm

Favorite Poem Project: www.favoritepoem.org/

Magnetic Poetry: home.freeuk.net/elloughton13/scramble.htm

Poetry Writing: teacher.scholastic.com/writewit/poetry/index.htm

Poetry Zone: www.poetryzone.ndirect.co.uk/index2.htm

Probability

Maths File: www.bbc.co.uk/education/mathsfile/

Using Data and Statistics: www.mathleague.com/help/data/data.htm

Probability: www.cut-the-knot.com/probability.html

Ken White's Coin Flipping Page: shazam.econ.ubc.ca/flip/index.html

Tables and Graphs:
pittsford.monroe.edu/jefferson/calfieri/graphs/TabGraphMain.html

Spelling

SpellCheck: www.funbrain.com/spell/index.html

SpellaRoo: www.funbrain.com/spellroo/

Harcourt Brace Spelling:
www.harcourtschool.com/menus/harcourt_brace_spelling.html

Spin and Spell: www.spinandspell.com/

Foreign Languages for Travelers: www.travlang.com/languages/

Tessellations and Symmetry

Symmetry and Pattern—The Art of Oriental Carpets:
mathforum.org/geometry/rugs/index.html

Hypercard and Tessellations: mathforum.org/sum95/suzanne/tess.html

Symmetry around the World: www.schools.ash.org.au/stkierans-manly/
Classes/Yr6/6B/Symmetry/index.htm

Totally Tessellated: http://library.thinkquest.org/16661/

Coolmath 4 Kids—Tessellations: www.coolmath4kids.com/tesspag1.html

Tongue Twisters

English Tongue Twisters: www.uebersetzung.at/twister/en.htm

Fun with Words!: library.thinkquest.org/J0111282/

The Tongue Twister Database:
www.geocities.com/Athens/8136/tonguetwisters.html

Tongue Twisters: www.fun-with-words.com/tong_explain.html

Very Silly Tongue Twisters: msowww.anu.edu.au/~ralph/tt.html

Volume

Converting U.S. Volume Units: www.aaamath.com/mea69-us-volume.html

Elementary Measurement:
mathforum.org/library/problems/sets/elem_measurement.html

WebQuest—Measuring Volume, Mass, and Weight:
www.sinc.sunysb.edu/Stu/bfields/webquest.html

Unit Conversion Calculators: www.cyberstation.net/~jweesner/conv.html

Weaving
An Archive of American Patchwork Quilt Designs: **womensearlyart.net/quilts**
del Corazon: **nmaa-ryder.si.edu/webzine/**
Colonial Crafts Workshop:
hastings.ci.lexington.ma.us/classroom/colonial/weaving.html
Republic of Ghana—Kente Cloth: **www.ghana.com/republic/kente/kente.html**
Kids' Corner Weaving Projects: **weavespindye.org/html/kids.html**

TEACHING TIPS   The learning activities in the Form and Structure theme focus on standards across the curriculum. Innovative teachers may use a number of strategies to integrate the subject matter with technology. Cooperative learning strategies, for example, provide an excellent opportunity for creative teachers to distribute technology resources throughout specific learning activities and groups. Similarly, teachers may use concept-attainment strategies and graphic organizers to introduce or present new ideas to the entire class.

LESSON EXTENDERS   Students could be instructed to look for "rule breakers" while working on the Form and Structure theme. Ordinarily they would be looking for structural patterns rather than looking for exceptions to the rules. However, much can be learned about the structure of patterns while analyzing the exceptions. For example, they could create lists of words that don't follow common spelling patterns. They could look for poetry or music that had been created by a "rule breaker" but where the piece of work was a success.

After sharing the tongue twister books with the younger buddy class, the students could teach their little buddies to create tongue twisters. This exercise would help to sharpen the phonological awareness of the younger students. The older students could then create another book on the computer, illustrating the younger students' tongue twisters.

Literature Patterns

Students will develop an understanding of the structure inherent in various genres of literature by reading selected books that contain common elements. The teacher may choose the genre to be fairy or folk tales, myths or fables, or related subjects.

STANDARDS MET IN THIS UNIT

NETS 1, 2, 3, 4
English Language Arts 1, 2, 3, 5, 6, 8, 12
Social Studies Ic

WEB RESOURCES

Fairy Tales
  Aesop's Fables—Traditional and Modern: **www.umass.edu/aesop**
  The Grimm Brothers: **www.nationalgeographic.com/grimm/**
  Myths, Folk Tales and Fairy Tales:
    teacher.scholastic.com/writewit/mff/fairytales_home.htm
  Absolutely Whootie—Stories to Grow By: **www.storiestogrowby.com**
  SurLaLune Fairy Tale Pages: **members.aol.com/surlalune/frytales/index.htm**

SOFTWARE

Access or Appleworks
Inspiration

DAYS 1 THROUGH 3

A variety of cultural variations of one particular story should be available for each group of students. For example, one group of students might read *Bigfoot Cinderrrrrella* by Tony Johnston and *Cindrillon: A Creole Cinderella* by Robert D. San Souci. Another group could read *Sootface: An Ojibwa Cinderella Story* by Robert D. San Souci and *The Golden Slipper: A Vietnamese Legend* by Darrell Lum, while another group reads *Chinye: A West African Folk Tale* by Obi Onyefulu and *The Golden Sandal: A Middle Eastern Cinderella* by Rebecca Hickox.

While some students are reading books, others can conduct Internet searches for other cultural variations. The students might search Yahooligans (www.yahooligans.com) for additional cultural variations of their chosen fairy tale, myth, or fable by going to the School Bell and Language Arts portion of the site. If time is an issue, teachers might want to preselect sites and even possibly bookmark them for easy access by students.

Some suggested Web sites to bookmark:

  Aesop's Fables Online Collection: **www.pacificnet.net/~johnr/aesop/**
  Aesop's Fables—Traditional and Modern: **www.umass.edu/aesop**
  Cinderella: **www.hiyah.com/library/cinderella.html**
  Absolutely Whootie—Stories to Grow By: **www.storiestogrowby.com**

DAY 4   Students should work in their groups to brainstorm similarities and differences within the stories. Use chart paper, word processing software (outline format), or Inspiration to record the findings.

DAYS 5 AND 6   Based upon the results of the brainstorming activity, database fields can be determined with guidance from the teacher. Either the teacher or the student groups can create a database containing appropriate fields. Using Cinderella variations as an example, fields could include the main character, the setting, chores, the source of magic, the "meanies," the type of fruit or vegetable turned into a coach, the type of animal turned into horses, the type of animal turned into the coachman, the ending, and so on.

DAYS 7 AND 8   Students will enter data into the fields of the database. They might need to refer to their books or the Internet sites to find selected information to fit the fields of the database. The groups can compare results and discuss the structure or pattern of their chosen story.

DAYS 9 THROUGH 12   Students will create their own stories based upon the genre of literature they have been studying. Original stories can be typed on a word processor, illustrated with drawing tools, and bound in book format for a class book.

ASSESSMENT   Develop an assessment rubric that covers the following criteria, adding your own criteria:

Content
- original story follows the fairy tale structure
- spelling
- grammar
- neatness
- creativity
- bound in book format

Technology
- use of database
- text formatting
- original drawings
- importing of graphics
- saved digital copies of student work

The teacher can create the rubric or have students create a rubric in cooperative groups. It is best to have the rubric available at the beginning of the project so that the students know what is expected of them. Students can self-assess or assess one or two other group efforts, and the teacher can use the same rubric for assessment purposes. For help in creating rubrics, use as a resource Chapter 5, "Constructing a Rubric," in Section 1, Strategies for Getting Started.

Dance Patterns

In this unit, students incorporate the use of math and technology skills to produce original dance sequences. They learn to understand the patterns associated with dancing and to produce QuickTime movies.

STANDARDS MET IN THIS UNIT

NETS 1, 2, 3
English Language Arts 4, 8
Social Studies Ic, IXa
Math 2

WEB RESOURCES

Dance
African Music and Dance Ensemble:
    www.cnmat.berkeley.edu/~ladzekpo/Ensemble.html
Early Break Dancing: www.americaslibrary.gov/pages/jp_dance_break_1.html
ThinkQuest Journey to New Worlds, Hula:
    tqjunior.thinkquest.org/6073/hawnres/hrhula.html
Let's Dance Latin Style!: library.thinkquest.org/J002194F/
The Shanghai Acrobatic Troupe: www.shanghaiacrobats.com

SOFTWARE

HyperStudio
PowerPoint
QuickTime or iMovie

DAYS 1 AND 2

The teacher will select dance videotapes that clearly show examples of rhythmic dance patterns. Tapes might include artists such as Tap Dogs, Stomp, Gregory Hines, or Savion Glover or could include examples from various ethnic dance groups. Excerpts from the videotapes will be shown to the whole class. Students will watch for patterns on the dance videotapes. They will learn how music is "counted" and how dances are frequently composed of a series of repeated patterns followed by a break. If time allows, students might also watch short QuickTime dance movies on Internet sites such as Time Step! at www.ukjtd.force9.co.uk/Timestepsite/.

DAYS 3 THROUGH 5

The students will work in small groups to compose their own short rhythmic dance sequences. Their final efforts can be videotaped using a digital video camera.

DAYS 6 THROUGH 7

Use the digital video camera and QuickTime or iMovie to create QuickTime movies that can be saved to a server or the hard drive of the classroom computers.

DAYS 8 THROUGH 10

QuickTime movie sequences of student dance performance patterns can be inserted into a multimedia presentation. Certain slides or cards could have the imported movies while other slides or cards could contain a textual and audio explanation of the structure of the dance patterns shown in the movies.

ASSESSMENT   Develop an assessment rubric that covers the following criteria, adding your own criteria:

Content
- evidence of dance patterns from different traditions
- use of rhythm
- use of music
- use of costume
- dance composition

Technology
- use of digital video camera
- video editing
- import video into multimedia application
- saved digital copies of student work

For help in creating rubrics, use as a resource the "Constructing a Rubric" essay found in the Strategies for Getting Started chapter of this book.

Fabric Patterns

In this unit, students learn that geometric patterns in fabric designs are an interesting phenomenon to explore both in books and on the Internet. Choose a culture or cultures that have significance within the grade level curriculum. Examples offered here include African Kente cloth, Navajo weavings, and quilts from America or India.

STANDARDS MET IN THIS UNIT
NETS 1, 3, 4
English Language Arts 8
Social Studies Ic, IXa
Math 3

WEB RESOURCES
Weaving
An Archive of American Patchwork Quilt Designs: womensearlyart.net/quilts
del Corazon: nmaa-ryder.si.edu/webzine/
Colonial Crafts Workshop:
    hastings.ci.lexington.ma.us/classroom/colonial/weaving.html
Republic of Ghana—Kente Cloth: www.ghana.com/republic/kente/kente.html
Kids' Corner Weaving Projects: weavespindye.org/html/kids.html

SOFTWARE
Microsoft Draw/Paint or Appleworks

DAY 1
Students will read or hear stories such as *Kofi and His Magic* by Maya Angelou, or Kente Colors, by Debbi Chocolate. All students may read or hear the same story or you might choose to divide students into cooperative groups with each group reading a different story.

DAYS 2 AND 3
Teachers who feel comfortable allowing their students to conduct Internet searches can explain search techniques using keywords such as kente, quilts, or "Navajo weavings" in Yahooligans, Yahoo, Dogpile, or a different search engine. If time is an issue, teachers might want to preselect sites and even possibly bookmark them for easy access by students. Some suggested sites to bookmark:

Navajo weaving sites
    First Nation/Fine Weavers: www.westfolk.org/exhibits.weavers.html
    Navajo Rugs: www.canyonart.com/rugs.htm
Kente cloth sites
    Republic of Ghana—Kente Cloth: www.ghana.com/republic/kente/kente.html
    Kente is More than a Cloth: http://users.erols.com/kemet/kente.htm
    Akan Kente Cloths: www.marshall.edu/akanart/cloth_kente.html
Quilt sites
    Quilts from India: www.shalincraft-india.com/decor3.html

Texana Quilt Company (America):
http://texanaquiltcompany.com/index.html?source=goto

Students should sketch the designs that they like from the sites they visit. They will need paper, pencils, and clipboards. As with learning to take notes, they will need guidance to learn how to sketch (rather than spending time drawing a perfect example of a design) and they should take note of appropriate color options. Some sites explain the cultural significance of certain color choices, too.

DAYS 4 AND 5 Have students use a computer drawing or painting program to create fabric designs based upon information from their reading and their Internet research. Students may need instruction first in copying and pasting and in drawing straight lines or using the circle, rectangle, and fill tools in their drawing program. The students will create a fabric design using some of the geometric repeated patterns that they sketched from their Internet research. There should first be a class or group discussion of possible color choices so students will select colors that would normally be used by the particular culture.

DAY 6 Student work can be printed and assembled into a class book or added to a word processing document or multimedia presentation offering an explanation of the cultural significance of the designs. They could also be printed onto special iron-on "paper" and actually ironed onto fabric such as handkerchiefs. Students can also use household materials and weave them together to create fashion accessories and wall hangings. Students could then do a short oral presentation while sharing their creations with the class.

ASSESSMENT Develop an assessment rubric that covers the following criteria, adding your own criteria:

Content
- evidence of culturally appropriate patterns
- use of culturally appropriate colors
- neatness
- creativity
- aesthetics

Technology
- use a draw program
- draw straight lines
- draw proportional shapes
- use copy, paste and fill functions in a draw program

For help in creating rubrics, use as a resource the "Constructing a Rubric" essay found in the Strategies for Getting Started chapter of this book.

Tessellation Patterns

Students will be introduced to the artistic and mathematical properties of tessellations by viewing, manipulating, and writing about tessellations that appear in everyday life.

STANDARDS MET IN THIS UNIT

NETS 1, 3, 4
English Language Arts 4, 5, 6, 7, 8
Math 3

WEB RESOURCES

Tessellations and Symmetry
  Symmetry and Pattern—The Art of Oriental Carpets:
    mathforum.org/geometry/rugs/index.html
  Hypercard and Tessellations: mathforum.org/sum95/suzanne/tess.html
  Symmetry around the World: www.schools.ash.org.au/stkierans-manly/
    Classes/Yr6/6B/Symmetry/index.htm
  Totally Tessellated: http://library.thinkquest.org/16661/
  Coolmath 4 Kids—Tessellations: www.coolmath4kids.com/tesspag1.html

Online Art Galleries
  Art on the Net: www.art.net/
  Eschart and Illusions: www.domaindlx.com/Escher/
  The Museum of Modern Art, New York: moma.org/
  Tessellating Animation: www18.big.or.jp/~mnaka/home.index.html
  Webmuseum, Paris: www.ibiblio.org/wm/

SOFTWARE

TesselMania Deluxe
Word or Appleworks

DAYS 1 THROUGH 3

Visit the following sites about M. C. Escher and Makoto Nakamura. The teacher can present these sites to a full class using one computer with a large-screen TV or projection device and then allow time for questions or discussion.

M.C. Escher
  Eschart and Illusions: www.domaindlx.com/Escher/

Makoto Nakamura
  Tessellating Animation: www18.big.or.jp/~mnaka/home.index.html

DAY 4

The teacher can present a lesson about the mathematical properties of tessellations by leading students in a discussion about tessellations in nature and daily life (pineapples, fish scales, tile floors, etc.). They should also discuss types of polygons that can tessellate and predict why some don't tessellate on a plane. The teacher can then introduce the concept of reflectional, transitional, and rotational transformations. The Tessellate! Web site can be used by the teacher to provide background information about types of symmetry, transformations, tessellations in daily life, and related topics: www.shodor.org/interactivate/activities/tessellate.

DAYS 5 AND 6 Students can try altering the variables of color, shape, and type of symmetry to design tessellations of their own while visiting the Tessellate! interactive site: www.shodor.org/interactivate/activities/tessellate.

Or students could use TesselMania Deluxe software if it is available. Allow enough time for all students to have an opportunity to try tessellations with various shapes of polygons and a variety of color combinations. They should take note of their favorite designs and how they were created.

DAY 6 Students should now save a copy of their favorite tessellation into a word processing program or multimedia application (see directions given at the site for importing and printing designs). The students can then write and present their understanding of the mathematics behind their creations.

ASSESSMENT Develop an assessment rubric that covers the following criteria, adding your own criteria:

Content
- evidence of tessellation
- evidence of symmetry
- evidence of transformation
- neatness
- aesthetics

Technology
- manipulate digital tessellations
- alter color, shape and symmetry of digital tessellations
- create a digital tessellation
- import a tessellation into an application

For help in creating rubrics, use as a resource the "Constructing a Rubric" essay found in the Strategies for Getting Started chapter of this book.

Music Patterns

Students will explore rhythmic music patterns from a multicultural perspective. Afterward, they will create their own musical sequence and present it with digital video.

STANDARDS MET IN THIS UNIT

NETS 1, 2, 3
English Language Arts 4, 8
Social Studies Ic, IXa
Math 2

WEB RESOURCES

Music
CBC 4 Kids—Music: www.cbc4kids.ca/general/music/
Music Genre Sampler: datadragon.com/education/genres/
STOMP—Percussion for Kids: www.stomponline.com/percuss1.html
Turntables: www.turntables.de/start.htm#

SOFTWARE

HyperStudio
PowerPoint
QuickTime or iMovie

DAYS 1 AND 2

The teacher will select music videotapes, audiotapes, or CDs that clearly show examples of rhythmic music patterns. Tapes could include examples from various ethnic music groups. Excerpts from the videotapes, audiotapes, or CDs will be played for the whole class. Students will listen for patterns. They will learn how music is "counted."

DAYS 3 THROUGH 5

The students will work in small groups to compose their own short rhythmic music sequences. Their final efforts can be videotaped using a digital video camera. (If the teacher does not have access to a digital video camera, proceed to the next step. The final efforts will be recorded directly into their multimedia presentations.) Note: This can be done in concert with the dance unit for this theme.

DAYS 6 AND 7

Use the digital video camera and QuickTime or iMovie to create QuickTime movies that can be saved to a server or the hard drive of the classroom computers.

DAYS 8 THROUGH 10

Videotapes of student music performance patterns can be inserted into Multimedia presentations along with their recorded explanations of the patterns. If the teacher did not have a digital video camera, then the students could create their slides or stacks and start with the textual explanations of the patterns. Rather than inserting a QuickTime movie, the students could record themselves playing the musical sequences directly into the multimedia presentation by playing their patterns with the microphone on.

ASSESSMENT   Develop an assessment rubric that covers the following criteria, adding your own criteria:

Content
- evidence of music patterns from different traditions
- use of rhythm
- use of music
- use of costume
- music composition

Technology
- use of digital video camera
- video editing
- import video into multimedia application
- saved digital copies of student work

For help in creating rubrics, use as a resource the "Constructing a Rubric" essay found in the Strategies for Getting Started chapter of this book.

Model Patterns

Students will combine their understanding of form, structure, and pattern to create various physical models. Working in cooperative groups, students research on the Internet and use digital cameras to record the progress of their project.

STANDARDS MET IN THIS UNIT

NETS 1, 2, 3, 4, 5, 6
English Language Arts 4, 7, 8
Math 4
Science E1, E2, E3 (K–4); E1, E2 (5–8)

WEB RESOURCES

Models
 Ask ERIC, Building Bridges: http://askeric.org/cgi-bin/printlessons.cgi/
  Virtual/Lessons/Arts/Architecture/ARC0200.html
 Build It and Bust It: library.thinkquest.org/11686/
 Creative Classroom Online:
  www.creativeclassroom.org/mj00hotstuff/index2.html
 Look, Learn and Do: www.looklearnanddo.com/documents/home.html

Ask an Expert
 Pitsco's Ask an Expert: www.askanexpert.com
 CIESE Ask an Expert Sites: njnie.dl.stevens-tech.edu/askanexpert.html
 Focus Educational Services: www.studentsonly.net
 Kids Connect: www.ala.org/ICONN/AskKC.html
 WonderKorner: www.peak.org/~bonwritr/wonder1.htm

SOFTWARE

HyperStudio
PowerPoint
QuickTime or iMovie

DAYS 1 THROUGH 3

The students should form cooperative groups to read various books about how things are built (kites, bridges, boats, castles, missions, etc.). Each group could build something different or each group could build different types of the same structure. If students were studying flight in science, then kites could be an appropriate structure to build. If they were studying fairy tales in literature, then castles might be more appropriate. Students should take notes about (1) the materials needed to complete the structure and (2) the possible ways to assemble their structures.

While some students are doing their research in books, others might use the Internet. Allow enough time for all groups to spend some of their time at the computers while others are conducting research in books. If time permits, they could conduct Internet searches using keywords such as "kite building," "bridge building." If time is an issue, you might want to bookmark preselected sites, such as:

> Ask ERIC, Building Bridges: http://askeric.org/cgi-bin/printlessons.cgi/
> Virtual/Lessons/Arts/Architecture/ARC0200.html
> Creative Classroom Online:
> www.creativeclassroom.org/mj00hotstuff/index2.html
> Look, Learn and Do: www.looklearnanddo.com/documents/home.html

To clear up any confusion students may have about building their models, they could participate in one of the organized "ask the expert" programs by using either their own e-mail addresses or with the teacher sending group e-mails to the experts. Allow time for the experts to respond to the messages before proceeding. Suggested student-oriented expert sites include:

> Pitsco's Ask an Expert: www.askanexpert.com
> LookSmart Ask an Expert for Students:
> www.looksmart.com/eus1/eus53706/eus53720/eus53813/eus150946/r?l&t

Based upon their research in books and on the Internet, students should have a list of materials needed to construct their structures. Most items should be easy to find and inexpensive (such as toothpicks, string, Popsicle sticks, etc.). Depending upon the situation, they could write letters home requesting these supplies or the supplies could be ordered, in which case the next step will not take place until the supplies arrive.

DAYS 4 THROUGH 7 Students will work in their groups to build their models. The length of time to complete this activity varies with the complexity of the models. While each group is building its models, students should rotate through the role of photographer using a digital video camera or a digital camera to record the building process. A disposable camera could be used (if the teacher has access to a scanner) rather than a digital camera or video camera.

DAYS 8 THROUGH 10 Once the models have been built, the students can create multimedia presentations that offer photos or movies of the building process along with an explanation of the process. Each group could create a multimedia presentation as part of a larger class slide show.

ASSESSMENT Develop an assessment rubric that covers the following criteria, adding your own criteria:

Content
- researched model design
- documentation of each step of the model-building process
- use of common or household materials
- safe use of tools and materials
- neatness

Technology
- use of digital camera or video camera

- video editing
- import digital images and/or video into multimedia application
- use of buttons or transitions in presentation
- saved digital copies of student work

For help in creating rubrics, use as a resource the "Constructing a Rubric" essay found in the Strategies for Getting Started chapter of this book.

Poetry Patterns

Students will read various types of poetry to develop an understanding of the rhyming patterns involved. Poetry types might include haiku, limericks, cinquains, rhymed pairs, or others.

STANDARDS MET IN THIS UNIT

NETS 3
English Language Arts 1, 2, 3, 4, 5, 6, 8, 12

WEB RESOURCES

Poetry
Crazy Limerick Machine:
www.ambleside.schoolzone.co.uk/ambleweb/year4/limerick.htm
Favorite Poem Project: www.favoritepoem.org/
Magnetic Poetry: home.freeuk.net/elloughton13/scramble.htm
Poetry Writing: teacher.scholastic.com/writewit/poetry/index.htm
Poetry Zone: www.poetryzone.ndirect.co.uk/index2.htm

SOFTWARE

Word or Appleworks

DAYS 1 THROUGH 3

Each group could read a different type of poetry each day or all groups could read the same types each day. Provide an opportunity for whole group sharing of examples of the patterns. Use a word processing application to identify and label meter and rhyme scheme using text color, bold, italic and underline text formatting features.

While some students are reading poetry in books, other students might also go to Yahooligans, School Bell, Language Arts, and Poetry and then click on the section containing their selected type of poem. Create a collection of favorite poems by having students type and save them digitally.

DAYS 4 THROUGH 6

Students will create their own poems following the patterns of the poems they've read. Student writing can be done on a word processor, illustrated with drawing tools or clip art, and bound in book format for a class book.

ASSESSMENT

Develop an assessment rubric that covers the following criteria, adding your own criteria:

Content
- evidence of poetry structure
- evidence of attention to meter and rhyme scheme
- inclusion of different kinds of poetry
- neatness

- bound in book format

Technology
- text formatting

- original digital graphics

- importing of digital images

- saved digital copies of student work

For help in creating rubrics, use as a resource the "Constructing a Rubric" essay found in the Strategies for Getting Started chapter of this book.

Probability Patterns

Students participate in a class simulation to facilitate understanding of the patterns and predictive abilities associated with statistics. (Adapted from "Probability and Statistics," *Family Math*, pp. 140–141 (Stenmark, Thompson, and Cossey).

STANDARDS MET IN THIS UNIT

NETS 1, 2, 3, 5, 6
English Language Arts 4, 7, 8
Math 4
Science E1, E2, E3 (K–4); E1, E2 (5–8)

WEB RESOURCES

Probability
Maths File: www.bbc.co.uk/education/mathsfile/
Using Data and Statistics: www.mathleague.com/help/data/data.htm
Probability: www.cut-the-knot.com/probability.html
Ken White's Coin Flipping Page: shazam.econ.ubc.ca/flip/index.html
Tables and Graphs
Tables and Graphs:
pittsford.monroe.edu/jefferson/calfieri/graphs/TabGraphMain.html

SOFTWARE

Excel or Appleworks
HyperStudio
PowerPoint

DAY 1

To help students understand probability, have the students conduct the following simulation. A shirt manufacturing company wants to gather data for a new style of shirt and needs to know the arm length of students. The students' job is to measure the lengths of classmates' arms (from the point of the shoulder to wrist bones) and record the information using a chart provided by the teacher. On a chart similar to the one below, the students will then record how many students have each arm length. It will be important to extend the range of the chart beyond the shortest and longest arm length recorded for the class.

ARM LENGTH	50 cm	51 cm	52 cm	etc.
NUMBER OF STUDENTS	###	###	###	

DAY 2   Using the data gathered on Day 1, have the students enter the data from the handwritten chart into a spreadsheet. Then use the spreadsheet program's graphing function to create a line graph showing the data gathered.

DAY 3   Discuss the data gathered from the class measurements and help the class make some predictions about the arm lengths of their classmates in other rooms.

Using the data from Day 1, have the students predict the number of students for each arm length in a larger population of similar age or grade students. To do this, multiply both the number of students in the class and the number of students with each arm length by the same factor. This data should be recorded in a spreadsheet such as this:

	ENTIRE CLASS	48cm	49cm	50cm	51cm	52cm	etc.
NUMBER OF STUDENTS	25			2	3	4	
FACTOR	4			4	4	4	
PREDICTED #	100			8	12	16	
FACTOR	10			10	10	10	
PREDICTED #	250			20	30	40	

NOTE   *Help the students understand that, because students in the middle elementary grades grow so rapidly, it is important to control the age of the students as you expand the size of the group.*

After recording the predictions, use the spreadsheet program's graphing function to create another line graph with the students' predictions for the larger population.

DAY 4   Divide the students into smaller groups and send each group to a different class to record the arm lengths of a larger population of students of similar ages. When each group returns, they should record their data on a chart similar to this one:

Arm Length

	CLASS SIZE	50cm	51cm	50cm	52cm
OUR CLASS	25	2	3	4	
CLASS 2	26	3			
CLASS 3	etc.	etc.			
etc.	etc.				
TOTALS	104				

DAY 5 Add the new data (for the totals) to the spreadsheet from Day 3 and construct a new line graph that shows the students' predictions in one color and the actual data in a different color. Discuss the predictions and the actual results. Help the students understand how this type of prediction is used in marketing, political polling, and scientific research.

DAY 6 Introduce the concept of mean, median, and mode and help the students calculate each for the data gathered. Spreadsheets can calculate these statistics for the students, but it is important for students to understand how each is calculated. For an explanation of these, consult any math text.

DAYS 7 THROUGH 10 (OPTIONAL) Individuals or small groups of students could develop a multimedia presentation or "chart talk" that presents the findings of their group and discusses how their group's data compared with the larger group.

EXTENSION Ask students to predict the numbers for a large group, given the data for a small sample, and explain how they arrived at their predictions.

ASSESSMENT Develop an assessment rubric that covers the following criteria, adding your own criteria:

Content
- accurate recording of data
- use of mean, median, and mode
- predictions based on patterns of data
- neatness
- presentation

Technology
- use of a spreadsheet
- use of formulae
- creation of graphs
- importing spreadsheet into multimedia presentation

For help in creating rubrics, use as a resource the "Constructing a Rubric" essay found in the Strategies for Getting Started chapter of this book.

Word Patterns

Students identify the word patterns associated with tongue twisters and then create and illustrate their own twisters.

STANDARDS MET IN THIS UNIT
NETS 1, 3, 4
English Language Arts 1, 4, 5, 6, 8, 11, 12

WEB RESOURCES

Tongue Twisters
English Tongue Twisters: www.uebersetzung.at/twister/en.htm
Fun with Words!: library.thinkquest.org/J0111282/
The Tongue Twister Database:
   www.geocities.com/Athens/8136/tonguetwisters.html
Tongue Twisters: www.fun-with-words.com/tong_explain.html
Very Silly Tongue Twisters: msowww.anu.edu.au/~ralph/tt.html

SOFTWARE

Word or Appleworks

DAYS 1 AND 2

Students will read tongue twisters in books such as:

Faint Frogs Feeling Feverish and Other Terrifically Tantalizing Tongue Twisters
  by Lilian Obligado
Six Sleepy Sheep by Jeffie Ross Gordon
Peter Piper's Alphabet by Marcia Brown
Snowman Sniffles and Other Verse by N. M. Bodecker

Other groups of students might also go to Yahooligans (www.yahooligans.com) and click on Language Arts and then type in tongue twisters to conduct an internal search.

DAY 3

Students will create a word processing document that features their favorite tongue-twister or nonsense poem along with a digital graphic. This document will be saved digitally to be included in a class collection of tongue twisters.

DAY 4 AND 5

Students will create their own tongue twisters following the patterns discovered while reading books on tongue twisters. They can use illustrated word processing software such as Storybook Weaver Deluxe to produce their work. They should look over the available choices of characters and objects before writing so their illustrations can match their sentences. For example, they could illustrate "Pretty purple pigs pick pink pumpkins." Pages can be printed, assembled into a book, and given to a younger "buddy" class, or saved digitally and added to the class collection of tongue twisters.

ASSESSMENT Develop an assessment rubric that covers the following criteria, adding your own criteria:

Content
- evidence of tongue twister structure
- evidence of attention to meter and rhyme scheme
- inventive or playful use of language
- neatness
- bound in book format

Technology
- text formatting
- original digital graphics
- importing of digital images
- saved digital copies of student work

For help in creating rubrics, use as a resource the "Constructing a Rubric" essay found in the Strategies for Getting Started chapter of this book.

Volume Patterns: "The Soda Pop Project"

Students use geometry and database skills to determine which products offer the "best value" to consumers.

STANDARDS MET IN THIS UNIT

NETS 3, 5, 6
English Language Arts 4
Math 3, 4

WEB RESOURCES

Volume
  Converting U.S. Volume Units: www.aaamath.com/mea69-us-volume.html
  Elementary Measurement:
    mathforum.org/library/problems/sets/elem_measurement.html
  WebQuest—Measuring Volume, Mass, and Weight:
    www.sinc.sunysb.edu/Stu/bfields/webquest.html
  Unit Conversion Calculators: www.cyberstation.net/~jweesner/conv.html

SOFTWARE

Access or Appleworks
Excel or Appleworks
HyperStudio
PowerPoint

NOTE

Prior to beginning the activity, ask students to collect soft drink cups, the prices, and the advertised size name (e.g., large, super, and jumbo) for various sizes at different locations (a variety of fast food places, movie theaters, sports arenas, fairs, carnivals, etc.). The class will need several sets of cups (all sizes offered for sale) from all the locations.

DAY 1

Ask students to share their experiences about buying soft drinks. Help the students focus on their perceptions of the cost of the drinks, the different sizes of cups, and the names given the sizes by the vendors.

Get suggestions from the students for ways to determine the best value. Students may suggest a variety of methods. How can they use the data they collected to decide? What additional data do they need, and how can they collect the data?

DAY 2

Divide the students into groups, with each group receiving several sets of cups from several different vendors (e.g., small, medium, and large cups from a fast food restaurant, a movie theater, and a ballpark). Provide each group with a source of water, a measuring cup, and data record sheet. Ask students to determine and record the actual capacity of the different cups, along with the sales price, the price charged by the vendor, and the price per ounce. Prior to beginning the activity, the students should agree on standards for what constitutes a "full" cup.

DAYS 3 THROUGH 6 Have students transfer the data recorded from their data sheets to a database on the class computer. The data from each cup should be recorded in a new record. If it is not possible to record all data into a single shared database, it will be necessary to merge all the data into one database with the records from all groups.

DAYS 7 THROUGH 10 Each group should use its own data and the data from the rest of the class to sort records and decide which specific cup size and vendor provide the best and least value to the purchaser. The groups should prepare a written explanation of their inquiry: their method, the data they collected, the whole class data, the filters they used, their decisions, and the reasons for those decisions. Each group can then import its database information into a spreadsheet to create charts and graphs and prepare a slide show presentation summarizing its findings.

ASSESSMENT Develop an assessment rubric that covers the following criteria, adding your own criteria:

Content
- proper volume measurement
- analysis of data
- recommendations
- neatness
- presentation

Technology
- accurate entry of data into database
- creation of filters to sort data
- importing of database into spreadsheet
- multimedia slide show

For help in creating rubrics, use as a resource the "Constructing a Rubric" essay found in the Strategies for Getting Started chapter of this book.

Spelling Patterns

Students use Inspiration to chart and organize common spelling patterns. They compare English word patterns to word patterns found in a foreign language.

STANDARDS MET IN THIS UNIT

NETS 1, 3, 4
English Language Arts 6, 7, 8, 9
Social Studies Ic

WEB RESOURCES

Spelling
SpellCheck: www.funbrain.com/spell/index.html
SpellaRoo: www.funbrain.com/spellroo/
Harcourt Brace Spelling:
   www.harcourtschool.com/menus/harcourt_brace_spelling.html
Spin and Spell: www.spinandspell.com/
Foreign Languages for Travelers: www.travlang.com/languages/

SOFTWARE

HyperStudio
Inspiration
PowerPoint

DAYS 1 AND 2

Students will study spelling patterns in their grade level spelling books. They should make note of some of the most common patterns in English. Notes could be charted or categorized using Inspiration or chart paper during whole class discussion time.

DAYS 3 THROUGH 5

Next, the students can visit some of the foreign language sites on the Internet. They can go to Yahooligans (www.yahooligans.com) and click on School Bell, Language Arts, and Languages or go to these suggested sites:

Quia—Languages: www.quia.com/lang.html (Offers games and quizzes in 10 different languages)
Learn Spanish: www.lingolex.com/spanish.htm (For learning Spanish vocabulary related to themes)
Learn to Speak Swahili: www.pbs.org/wonders/Episodes/Epi2/2_cultr1.htm
Swahili: www.kent.wednet.edu/curriculum/soc_studies/kenya/swahili.html
Enchanted Learning: www.EnchantedLearning.com/Dictionary.html (Learn French, German, Portuguese, or Spanish)

They should look for spelling patterns in other languages. Each group of students might choose a different language. Students should chart on paper the spelling patterns that they discover in their selected foreign language. Allow time for discussion and comparison of foreign language spelling patterns with English spelling patterns.

DAY 6 Use a search engine to identify common misspellings of words on the World Wide Web. The students can work in their groups to create lists of the 10 most misspelled words they find online, or create a list of ten nonsense words. The structure of nonsense words should reflect the English and foreign language spelling patterns that the students discovered.

DAYS 7 AND 8 Using multimedia presentation software such as PowerPoint or HyperStudio, the students can create cards or slides for each of the words. Each slide or card should contain the sound of the students' voices reading the words, the word typed in a large font, and a picture of what the nonsense word "means" drawn with the drawing tools. All slides or cards could be linked to form a class show.

ASSESSMENT Develop an assessment rubric that covers the following criteria, adding your own criteria:

Content
- evidence of awareness of common spelling patterns in English
- evidence of awareness of common spelling patterns in a foreign language
- identification of common misspellings
- creation of nonsense words
- neatness
- presentation

Technology
- access of teacher-assigned Web sites
- use of Inspiration
- use of multimedia slide application
- use of buttons or transitions

For help in creating rubrics, use as a resource the "Constructing a Rubric" essay found in the Strategies for Getting Started chapter of this book.

culminating
event

Invention Convention

Each student selects one of his/her work products and showcases it at a day-long celebration of learning through Form and Structure. Students can present their work to one another in the morning, and then students from other classes can be scheduled in throughout the day to see student exhibits, and parents and the general community can be invited too.

Each student can set up an exhibit table with a display of his/her project, printed materials, work samples, and the chance to interact with interested visitors. Have students wear white lab coats for effect and have multimedia presentations playing via television or projector display at a central location for everyone to enjoy.

theme 2

BY SUSAN O'HARA AND MAUREEN MCMAHON

"Imagination is more important than knowledge."

—Albert Einstein

Imagination

Imagination is a theme that enriches and extends every form of learning that takes place in the classroom. As a concept, it takes learning of skills and concepts and gives it wings to soar to higher levels of cognition. Bloom's taxonomy could not address higher-level thinking if students were not able to combine the value of knowledge and comprehension with the power of synthesis and evaluation. The teacher who is able to foster imagination in his or her students by exploring and celebrating new ideas offers students more than the mastery of basic content. A fertile imagination can encounter unfamiliar ideas and make them its own. Indeed, imagination is the openness to new ideas.

Disney's work in the twentieth century is a model of how imagination can make use of technology to encourage everyone to dream. His work to transform fantasy into reality through film and theme parks helped society see new possibilities for creative expression. Also, his company's efforts to explore scientific and technological advances through exhibits such as Epcot Center helped expand the definition of creativity—it isn't just for the arts anymore! This theme affords students the chance to explore the genius of Disney by using modern-day digital technologies to learn and demonstrate their learning in creative ways.

The standards-based lessons in the following curriculum enable students to explore the concepts of imagination as they

- create fantasy characters by manipulating scanned images with drawing and painting software;

- write stories that come to life with inserted pictures and student drawings;

- make drawings of imaginary lands to scale using electronic grid or CAD programs;

- interpret the imagineering qualities of Walt Disney through analyses of his stories, movies, and theme parks;

- investigate and discuss cultural differences through the use of Internet resources to see the creative uniqueness resident in every culture;

- build electronic spreadsheets to better understand money's links to making imaginary ideas come to life; and

- explore animation through historical documentation, art, and the active creation of animated gifs.

Unit Tools

SPOTLIGHT ON
TECHNOLOGY

Designing Web Pages: In the Imagination and Culture unit, students create their own Web pages. Web page authoring is a fun activity for students and a great way for students to synthesize and present information. Using programs such as Claris Homepage and Netscape Composer makes Web design fun and feasible for even very young students. One of the most beneficial aspects of this activity is that students begin to think about presenting information in nonlinear ways and about using multimedia to present information and communicate ideas. Finally, students are very excited about creating their own Web pages and presenting them to others.

Creating and Editing Digital Movies: In the Imagineering Disney Style: Arts unit students create their own short movies. Students are excited when they get to use digital cameras and then edit movies on their computers using a program such as iMovie. Movie editing, which to many students seems like an incredibly complex task, suddenly becomes easy and feasible with this program. Once again students are exploring a new medium for communication, which helps them to think about the material in a different way.

Creating and Searching Databases: Database creation is a wonderful activity to do with your students. Creating databases helps students to think of numerous ways for organizing and categorizing information. It is fun and exciting to have students look at different information and to brainstorm some ways of sorting and creating categories for data. Also having students conduct Boolean searches in a database can help them prepare to conduct effective searches on the Internet.

Creating Multimedia Presentations: Students can use multimedia tools such as PowerPoint or HyperStudio to storyboard ideas before filmmaking, share original characters and stories, offer tours of countries and cultures, and even import digital movies as part of a larger presentation. Powerpoint has the added feature of being able to be transformed into a web page, so that student work can be presented as part of an online culminating event at the end of the theme.

Digital Semantic Mapping: Use of a semantic mapping tool such as Inspiration allows students the chance to generate a variety of ideas through its Rapid Fire function, or to visually arrange and sort ideas into different kinds of categories and hierarchies. Inspiration also allows them to import images and use links to create a more vibrant and interactive sharing of ideas. Inspiration maps can be saved as digital images and then presented in web pages.

CHILDREN'S
LITERATURE

Across Five Aprils by Irene Hunt
Bull Run by Paul Fleischman
Charlie and the Chocolate Factory by Roald Dahl
Charley Skedaddle by Patricia Beatty
Cloudy with a Chance of Meatballs by Judi Barrett
Goosebumps by R. L. Stine
How Much is a Million? by David M. Schwartz

TEACHER VOICES

If You Made a Million? by David M. Schwartz
It Looked Like Spilt Milk by Charles Shaw
James and the Giant Peach by Roald Dahl
Many Moons and The 13 Clocks by James Thurber
Mary Poppins by P.L. Travers
Regards to the Man on the Moon by Ezra Jack Keats
Round Trip by Ann Jonas
Stonewall by Jean Fritz
Where the Sidewalk Ends by Shel Silverstein
Selected Poems by Poet Laureate Rita Dove
The multitude of Ramona and Henry titles by Beverly Cleary
The many Dr. Seuss books, especially *Horton Hears a Who*

WRITING ACROSS
THE CURRICULUM

In the Imagineering Disney Style units, students could be asked to write a short, illustrated biography of Walt Disney. This biography could focus on Disney's use of imagination in his stories and movies.

In the Imagination and Culture unit students could write poetry that is reflective of their culture. They could also write an illustrated history of their culture.

In the Imagination and History lesson, students could write a letter from the trenches of war to a family member, describing what they are involved in and how they feel about the fighting.

TEACHER VOICES

About the Imagineering Units

"Walt Disney is characterized as the greatest imagineer of all time. Children are excited to study the art of imagination through the exploration of Walt Disney's stories, movies, songs, theme parks and memorabilia. They think they know Disney, until they begin uncovering information they never knew existed. The complex man behind Disneyland and Disneyworld is unveiled as the children use the Internet to read, view, and listen to primary source materials about the man and his imagination."

About the Imagine Yourself in History Unit

"Children's imaginations run rampant when they create fantasy characters by scanning in images of fictional characters and real people. They are able to build imaginary characters by using photo-editing software to mix the scanned-in media. Wow! The characters and stories they create are unbelievable. The technology seems to really release their creativity!"

WEB RESOURCES

Amusement Parks
Cedar Point: www.cedarpoint.com
Coney Island: www.pbs.org/wgbh/amex/coney/

Knott's Berry Farm: www.knotts.com
Six Flags: www.sixflags.com/home.asp
Tokyo Disney: www.tokyodisneyresort.co.jp/tdr/index_e.html

Animals
Animal World: www.kbears.com/animals.html
eNature.com: www.enature.com
NatureServe: www.natureserve.org
Virtual Zoo: www.lawrencegoetz.com/zoo/
World Wildlife Fund—Kid's Stuff: www.worldwildlife.org/fun/kids.cfm

Civil War
The American Civil War: http://tqjunior.thinkquest.org/5663/
The Civil War for Kids: www2.lhric.org/pocantico/civilwar/cwar.htm
Civil War Battlefield Images: www.geocities.com/civil_war_pics/
Civil War Sketchbook: www.gliah.uh.edu/sketchbook.html
Selected Civil War Photographs:
    http://memory.loc.gov/ammem/cwphtml/cwphome.html

Countries
Altapedia Online: www.atlapedia.com
Cultural Profiles Project: http://cwr.utoronto.ca/cultural/
Geographia: www.geographia.com
Infonation: www.un.org/Pubs/CyberSchoolBus/infonation/e_infonation.htm
Your Nation: www.your-nation.com

Cultures
The Bowers Kidseum: www.nativecreative.com/kidseum/frames.html
Cultural Connections: http://library.thinkquest.org/50055/index.shtml
Culture Quest World Tour: www.ipl.org/youth/cquest/
Global Gang: www.globalgang.org.uk/
Understanding Color: http://library.thinkquest.org/50065/

Disney
Disney Clip Art: www.disneyclipart.com
Disney Coloring Pages: http://disney.go.com/Kids/color/index.html
Disney Records Listening Center:
    http://asp.disney.go.com/DisneyRecords/ListeningCenter.asp
Disneyland: www.disneyland.com
ePals: www.epals.com
Forgotten Disney—The Lost Legacy: www.intercot.com/fdtll/
Hilda Taba—Inductive Thinking: http://ivc.uidaho.edu/mod/models/taba/
Imagineering.org: www.imagineering.org
Magic Kingdom Map:
    www.wdwinfo.com/wdwinfo/maps/WDW_Magic_Kingdom.jpg
Magic Kingdom Virtual Tour: www.geocities.com/mtcarmelplayers/
Virtual Guide to Walt Disney World:
    www.intercot.com/magickingdom/default.asp

Film Making
Cartoon Network: http://cartoonnetwork.com/doc/index.html
Cartoon Network—Animation "How To":
    www.cartoonnetwork.com/doc/animation_primer/index.html
Handbook for Storytellers: http://falcon.jmu.edu/~ramseyil/storyhandbook.htm
iMovie—Getting Started: www.apple.com/imovie/gettingstarted/
Storyboard: www.sotherden.com/video101/storyboard.htm

Grids and Coordinates
    Create a Graph: http://nces.ed.gov/nceskids/Graphing/
    General Coordinates Game:
       www.shodor.org/interactivate/activities/coords2/index.html
    Graphing Lesson Plans:
       www.teach-nology.com/teachers/lesson_plans/math/graphing/
    Introduction to the Coordinate Plane and Coordinates Discussion:
       www.shodor.org/interactivate/discussions/fd2.html
    Maps: http://pittsford.monroe.edu/jefferson/calfieri/maps&globes/Maps.html
Storytelling
    The Art of Storytelling: http://library.thinkquest.org/J001779/index.html
    Literature—What Makes a Good Short Story?:
       www.learner.org/exhibits/literature/
    Page by Page: www.nlc-bnc.ca/pagebypage/
    StoryQuest: http://tqjunior.thinkquest.org/5115/
    Storytelling Power: www.storytellingpower.com

TEACHING TIPS

Most of these lessons will work best if you employ cooperative learning group techniques. Additionally, these lessons are not designed for all students to do all parts of the lesson. Divide the students into groups and allow the student groups to choose an angle or task that most interests them. Following each group's work, facilitate sharing and understanding between groups. If time permits, student groups should be challenged to synthesize all other groups' work to prepare an end product of the students' or teacher's choosing.

LESSON EXTENDERS

Having students create their own mini theme park could extend the Imagineering Disney Style: Mathematics unit. Teams could create characters, attractions, restaurants, stores, and other features based on a set budget. Students could design a brochure to advertise their new theme park and put together a Web-based virtual tour of the park.

The Imagination and History unit could be extended by having students create a newspaper from the period they are studying. Using primary source materials from the Library of Congress Digital Archives, students could include pictures and accounts of a specific event that occurred during that time period. Each team could choose a different event for the focus of an illustrated article or letter, which could all be submitted to the newspaper.

Imagineering Disney Style: Science

Imagine studying Walt Disney and Disney enterprises as a way to view and understand the concept of imagination. Students will be challenged to interpret art, analyze the theme park layouts, discuss marketing issues, delve into literature about Walt Disney the man, listen to Disney music, and critique Disney films, all to gain a better understanding of the role imagination plays in making the "magic" happen in Disney endeavors. Students will develop an understanding of the characteristics of Disney's animals and how they are different from real animals. They will develop an understanding of animal characterization and classification.

STANDARDS MET IN THIS UNIT	NETS 2, 3, 4, 5, 6 English Language Arts 1, 3, 4, 6, 7, 8, 9, 12 Science A1, A2, C1, C2, C3

WEB RESOURCES	**Animals** Animal World: www.kbears.com/animals.html eNature.com: www.enature.com NatureServe: www.natureserve.org Virtual Zoo: www.lawrencegoetz.com/zoo/ World Wildlife Fund—Kid's Stuff: www.worldwildlife.org/fun/kids.cfm **Countries** Altapedia Online: www.atlapedia.com Cultural Profiles Project: http://cwr.utoronto.ca/cultural/ Geographia: www.geographia.com Infonation: www.un.org/Pubs/CyberSchoolBus/infonation/e_infonation.htm Your Nation: www.your-nation.com

SOFTWARE	Inspiration Microsoft Draw/Paint or Appleworks Word or Appleworks

DAY 1	In teams, students will explore Disney's animals. They will begin by watching some clips from famous Disney movies and reading Disney storybooks. In a brainstorming session, students will list as many Disney animals as they can remember. They will discuss their favorite Disney animals and what characteristics of these animals they particularly like.
DAY 2	Students will divide into smaller groups. One group will conduct research on the Internet to start listing characteristics of Disney animals. The other group will conduct research on the Internet to start listing characteristics of real animals. Students will be asked what characteristics they think the Disney animals have. They will discuss the unique personalities that the Disney animals have. Students

will then begin to brainstorm some fields for a database, facilitated by the teacher. Chart paper, word processing software, or Inspiration can be used to record findings.

DAY 3 Students will enter data in the database. Through database use and interpretation, students will begin to develop an understanding of animal characteristics and classification. Students will also use the database to conduct some searches. They will compare and contrast between the different Disney animals. Students will also compare and contrast between Disney animal personalities and real animal personalities. They will discuss how Walt Disney used imagination through the art of drawing and animation to transform real animals into Disney animals with their own unique personalities.

DAY 4 Students will write a personification of the animal they have entered into the database, giving it personality traits they usually attribute to people. This will be typed and saved as a word processing document.

DAY 5 Students will draw an original picture of the animal they have personified, including human traits. The drawing will be added to the description they have already saved as a word processing document.

ASSESSMENT Develop an assessment rubric that covers the following criteria, adding your own criteria:

Content

- evidence of traits of animals found in nature
- personification of animal
- caricature of personified animal
- neatness
- presentation

Technology
- use of database as an organizational tool
- use of word processing as a writing tool
- use of drawing application
- importing original graphics into word processing document
- saving completed file in digital format

For help in creating rubrics, use as a resource the "Constructing a Rubric" essay found in the Strategies for Getting Started chapter of this book.

Imagineering Disney Style: Social Studies

Students will develop a detailed classification process to analyze Disney's six "lands" for their cultural characteristics. Students will then use this process to analyze different cultures in the real world.

STANDARDS MET IN THIS UNIT	NETS 3, 5, 6 English Language Arts 4, 5, 11, 12 Social Studies Ia–e

WEB RESOURCES

Countries
Altapedia Online: www.atlapedia.com
Cultural Profiles Project: http://cwr.utoronto.ca/cultural/
Geographia: www.geographia.com
Infonation: www.un.org/Pubs/CyberSchoolBus/infonation/e_infonation.htm
Your Nation: www.your-nation.com

Disney
Disneyland: www.disneyland.com
ePals: www.epals.com
Hilda Taba–Inductive Thinking: http://ivc.uidaho.edu/mod/models/taba/
Imagineering.org: www.imagineering.org
Magic Kingdom Map:
www.wdwinfo.com/wdwinfo/maps/WDW_Magic_Kingdom.jpg
Magic Kingdom Virtual Tour: www.geocities.com/mtcarmelplayers/
Virtual Guide to Walt Disney World:
www.intercot.com/magickingdom/default.asp

SOFTWARE

Inspiration
Microsoft Draw/Paint or Appleworks
Word or Appleworks

DAY 1

Online, students explore Fantasyland, Adventureland, Frontierland, Tomorrowland, Critter Country, and Mickey's Toontown. Using chart paper, outline mode in Word, or Inspiration, they list characteristics that make each of the lands unique. As a group, they discuss how imagination surfaces within the cultural characteristics of each land.

DAY 2

Using a word-processing table builder, students will develop a Hilda Taba model for cultural prediction and identification. The Hilda Taba model is a classification process that involves three stages. First, students make a list of observations, ideas, or concepts. Second, students group similar items together. Third, students label each category. For more information and illustrative examples, go to http://ivc.uidaho.edu/mod/models/taba/.

DAY 3   Given a specific attraction, students will use the Taba model to identify which land the attraction belongs to. Using a graphic program, each student will build his or her own attraction, labeling its characteristics. The group must then predict which land this attraction would be built in.

DAY 4   Students will conduct research on the Internet on cultural differences across the world. Each student will choose a country to visit on the Web and list some characteristics of its culture that are unique. Using e-pals, students will communicate with their peers in France and Japan to discuss how Disneyland in their countries are culturally different. (Note: this e-mail arrangement must be set up by the teacher ahead of time.) As a group, the students will then engage in a discussion linking Disney's lands and their cultures with complex cultures of the world.

DAY 5   Students create a class Hilda Taba model in a word processing table that compares world cultures they have studied.

ASSESSMENT   Develop an assessment rubric that covers the following criteria, adding your own criteria:

Content
- amusement park cultures
- world cultures
- Hilda Taba model
- neatness
- organization

Technology
- use of tables in word processing
- use of WWW resources
- use of Inspiration
- use of drawing application

For help in creating rubrics, use as a resource the "Constructing a Rubric" essay found in the Strategies for Getting Started chapter of this book.

Imagineering Disney Style: Mathematics

Students will develop graphing skills and learn about the concept of scale by using an online map of Disneyland. They then explore how the concept of scale is used in movie making.

STANDARDS MET IN THIS UNIT

NETS 3, 5

English Language Arts 1, 3, 4, 7, 8, 11

Math 2, 3, 4, 6, 8, 9

Social Studies IIIa, c

WEB RESOURCES

Grids and Coordinates

Create a Graph: http://nces.ed.gov/nceskids/Graphing/

General Coordinates Game:
www.shodor.org/interactivate/activities/coords2/index.html

Graphing Lesson Plans:
www.teach-nology.com/teachers/lesson_plans/math/graphing/

Introduction to the Coordinate Plane and Coordinates Discussion:
www.shodor.org/interactivate/discussions/fd2.html

Maps: http://pittsford.monroe.edu/jefferson/calfieri/maps&globes/Maps.html

Disney

Disneyland: www.disneyland.com

Imagineering.org: www.imagineering.org

Magic Kingdom Map:
www.wdwinfo.com/wdwinfo/maps/WDW_Magic_Kingdom.jpg

Virtual Guide to Walt Disney World:
www.intercot.com/magickingdom/default.asp

SOFTWARE

Microsoft Draw/Paint or Appleworks

DAY 1

Using the Internet, students will find an online map of Disneyland. Once the students have downloaded the map, they will print it. Students will glue their map pieces onto a poster board. As a group, students will construct a grid on the map. They will use a marker to draw grid boxes on their Disneyland map, labeling the bottom squares (x-axis) with the letters of the alphabet and the side squares (y-axis) with numbers. At the bottom of the poster board, students will write down coordinates for five locations found on their grid. Other teams of students will be asked to use the coordinate pairs to identify the locations.

DAY 2

Using a drawing application with a grid the teacher has prepared ahead of time, students will draw Disney's five lands to scale.

Students will learn how to construct a diagram of the lands using symbols to represent attractions and a map legend. Teachers may also wish to incorporate the use of a compass rose into this activity. Students will then be asked to give directions between two locations in the park using coordinate pairs.

DAY 3   Students will explore the Internet for information about the use of scale in drawings and movie making. They will read some Walt Disney quotes on his own use of scale in developing his characters. If time is an issue, teachers might want to preselect sites and even bookmark them for easy access by students. As a group, students will engage in discussions on the relationship between scale and the power and magic of Walt Disney's imagination.

DAY 4   Use the personified animals from the Disney Social Studies unit and draw them to a life-sized scale. Teacher and students can determine what the life-sized dimensions should be. It is especially rewarding to have students create original characters that match their own height and proportions.

DAY 5   Using a drawing application and a grid, students will map out a plan for a classroom theme park that is drawn to scale based on the classroom's actual dimensions. Students can work individually or in small groups to create their plans. The class can then view each plan and vote on the best layout for a classroom theme park.

ASSESSMENT   Develop an assessment rubric that covers the following criteria, adding your own criteria:

Content
- understanding of a grid map
- accurate use of coordinates
- use of legends and symbols
- drawing to scale
- neatness

Technology
- use of drawing application
- use of rulers to create digital grids
- use of copy, cut and paste functions
- WWW research

For help in creating rubrics, use as a resource the "Constructing a Rubric" essay found in the Strategies for Getting Started chapter of this book.

Imagineering Disney Style: Language Arts and Storytelling

Students learn about the art of storytelling and how storytelling is an integral part of different cultures. Students then develop their own illustrated stories.

STANDARDS MET IN THIS UNIT

NETS 2, 3, 5
English Language Arts 1, 2, 3, 4, 5, 7, 8, 9, 11, 12
Social Studies Ia–e

WEB RESOURCES

Storytelling
   The Art of Storytelling: http://library.thinkquest.org/J001779/index.html
   Literature–What Makes a Good Short Story?:
      www.learner.org/exhibits/literature/
   Page by Page: www.nlc-bnc.ca/pagebypage/
   StoryQuest: http://tqjunior.thinkquest.org/5115/
   Storytelling Power: www.storytellingpower.com

SOFTWARE

HyperStudio
Inspiration
PowerPoint

DAY 1

Within their teams, students will give a personal recounting of their favorite Disney story. They will discuss the characteristics of the story that make it their favorite. As a team they will read one chosen Disney story and examine the role illustrations and words play in bringing the story to life and creating magic. As a group they will read some Walt Disney quotes on the writing of these stories.

DAY 2

Students will research the art of storytelling on the Internet, and they will discuss and develop an understanding of the role imagination plays in great storytelling. They will research and discuss the role storytelling has played in many cultures across the world, looking specifically at Native American storytelling. If time is an issue, teachers might want to preselect sites and even bookmark them for easy access by students.

DAY 3

Students web ideas for stories in Inspiration. The web must contain all the elements of a story and give details for each element: setting, characters, plot, conflict, resolution, and conclusion.

DAYS 4 AND 5

In groups, students will create their own illustrated stories using a multimedia program. They will present their stories to the class and discuss how they used multimedia and their imaginations to bring their ideas to life.

ASSESSMENT   Develop an assessment rubric that covers the following criteria, adding your own criteria:

Content
- evidence of story elements
- storytelling strategies
- author's voice
- illustration
- neatness
- creativity

Technology
- WWW research
- use of Inspiration
- use of multimedia application
- use of copy, cut and paste functions

For help in creating rubrics, use as a resource the "Constructing a Rubric" essay found in the Strategies for Getting Started chapter of this book.

Imagineering Disney Style: Arts

Students will explore the use of color in Disney's illustrations, books, and films.
They also examine the use of music as an artistic devise.

**STANDARDS MET
IN THIS UNIT**

NETS 2, 3, 4
English Language Arts 4, 5
Social Studies IXa

WEB RESOURCES

Disney
Disney Coloring Pages: http://disney.go.com/Kids/color/index.html
Film Making
Cartoon Network: http://cartoonnetwork.com/doc/index.html
Cartoon Network—Animation "How To":
   www.cartoonnetwork.com/doc/animation_primer/index.html
Handbook for Storytellers: http://falcon.jmu.edu/~ramseyil/storyhandbook.htm
iMovie—Getting Started: www.apple.com/imovie/gettingstarted/
Storyboard: www.sotherden.com/video101/storyboard.htm

SOFTWARE

HyperStudio
iMovie
Microsoft Draw/Paint or Appleworks
PowerPoint

**DAY 1
(VISUAL ARTS)**

In groups, students will import Disney coloring pages (http://disney.go.com/Kids/color/index.html) into a paint program and experiment with color choice. A class discussion will be held about how color affects human response and hence the magic. Students will use a draw program to create their own illustrations, experimenting with the use of different colors to achieve different effects.

**DAY 2
(MUSIC)**

Students will explore and discuss how music is used to enhance the animated characters in Disney movies. They will watch some movie clips and examine uses of speed, rhythm, and choice of instruments. Using an animation program, students will experiment with interchanging music with Disney characters to explore the effect of music.

DAY 3

Students study the storyboarding process and storyboard their story in preparation for creating a digital film. Storyboarding can be done on slides or cards in a multimedia program.

DAYS 4 AND 5

In groups, students will use iMovie to create and edit their own digital movie clips. They will experiment with different movie effects, transitions, and audio effects.

ASSESSMENT Students will discuss their personal uses of effects and sound to create magic in their movies.

Develop an assessment rubric that covers the following criteria, adding your own criteria:

Content
- evidence of story elements
- storytelling strategies
- storyboarding
- neatness
- creativity

Technology
- use of paint program
- use of digital music
- use of iMovie
- quality of slides/cards in multimedia program

For help in creating rubrics, use as a resource the "Constructing a Rubric" essay found in the Strategies for Getting Started chapter of this book.

Imagination and Culture

This is a five-day interdisciplinary unit. As students explore similarities between cultures across the world, they begin to develop an understanding of how different cultures exist and survive. Math, science, social studies, language arts, art, and technology are all woven together as groups of students each design their own culture model and create a Web-based virtual tour of this model.

STANDARDS MET IN THIS UNIT

NETS 2, 3, 4, 5, 6
English Language Arts 1, 2, 7, 8, 9, 11, 12
Social Studies Ia–e; IIa–f; IIIa, b, g, j, k; IVe, f

WEB RESOURCES

Cultures
The Bowers Kidseum: www.nativecreative.com/kidseum/frames.html
Cultural Connections: http://library.thinkquest.org/50055/index.shtml
Culture Quest World Tour: www.ipl.org/youth/cquest/
Global Gang: www.globalgang.org.uk/
Understanding Color: http://library.thinkquest.org/50065/

Amusement Parks
Cedar Point: www.cedarpoint.com
Coney Island: www.pbs.org/wgbh/amex/coney/
Knott's Berry Farm: www.knotts.com
Six Flags: www.sixflags.com/home.asp
Tokyo Disney: www.tokyodisneyresort.co.jp/tdr/index_e.html

SOFTWARE

HyperStudio
Microsoft Draw/Paint or Appleworks
Powerpoint

DAYS 1 AND 2

Students will research various cultures through virtual field trips and Internet exploration and will discuss and chart similarities and differences. They will bring the data they have gathered back to the class as a whole. A discussion will be held about cultural traditions and what they mean. Students will examine similarities and differences between cultures and begin to identify the ways different cultures meet basic human needs. In their groups, they will discuss traditions associated with their own cultural backgrounds. Through e-pals, each student will communicate with peers in different countries to discuss cultural similarities and differences. Students will explore the different components of various culture models.

DAYS 3 THROUGH 5

Students will divide into smaller collaborative groups and develop a culture model. Using a graphic program, each collaborative group will create a cultural flag, motto, and emblem. Each collaborative group will design basic architecture, cultural dress, and settlement and use a word processing program to provide an illustrated description. The cultural model will also include a description of its cultural ethics and codes. Groups will create financial, communication, and transport systems for their model. Groups will also create a staple diet for their culture. As a culminating project, students will host a virtual Web-based tour of their culture.

DAYS 6 THROUGH 10

Students will work in small groups to develop an amusement park culture, including a flag, colors, architecture, dress, transportation, communication, ethics and codes. The culture will be presented in a multimedia application that can be shared with the entire class.

ASSESSMENT

Develop an assessment rubric that covers the following criteria, adding your own criteria:

Content
- evidence of understanding of culture
- comparisons of cultures
- evidence of understanding of traditions
- creation of culture model
- creation of amusement park culture
- neatness

Technology
- use of Virtual Field Trips
- use of e-mail
- use of drawing program
- use of multimedia application

For help in creating rubrics, use as a resource the "Constructing a Rubric" essay found in the Strategies for Getting Started chapter of this book.

Imagination and History

Students will become more familiar with photo and picture digital editing through the use of software and a scanner. They will be challenged to research and reflect on what it was like to participate in the Civil War through a free writing narrative activity. Certainly, it would be appropriate for students to use draw and paint software to further illustrate their historical fantasy narrative. Technology, history, and creative writing are integrated in this unit. The Civil War is only one possibility for this lesson. One could use any set of pictures that reflect a topic of interest. The important aspect to the lesson is to have real pictures to aid students in imagining what it would be like to be in that moment in time.

STANDARDS MET IN THIS UNIT	NETS 1, 3 English Language Arts 1, 5, 7, 8, 9, 11, 12 Social Studies IIa–f

WEB RESOURCES Civil War
The American Civil War: http://tqjunior.thinkquest.org/5663/
The Civil War for Kids: www2.lhric.org/pocantico/civilwar/cwar.htm
Civil War Battlefield Images: www.geocities.com/civil_war_pics/
Civil War Sketchbook: www.gliah.uh.edu/sketchbook.html
Selected Civil War Photographs:
    http://memory.loc.gov/ammem/cwphtml/cwphome.html

SOFTWARE iMovie
Photoshop or Paint Shop Pro
Word or Appleworks

DAY 1 Read a selection of Red Badge of Courage to the class and have them verbally reflect on how they would feel in such a different environment. Emphasize that the people who fought in the Civil War were very similar to them.

DAY 2 Share with the students a large selection of Civil War photographs from books or online at the National Digital Library of Congress. Students select a picture to use and replace one of the faces in the picture with their own picture using Photoshop, Paint Shop Pro or similar photo/picture editing software. Students are then challenged to write a story explaining what happens immediately before and after their picture was taken, paying close attention to how they feel.

DAY 3 In medium-sized groups (six to eight children), students share their picture and stories. As a class, discuss the importance to understanding history from the human perspective and not to limit our understanding to just facts and dates.

DAY 4   Students storyboard their stories and prepare any extra images to create an animated digital movie of the Civil War event they selected.

DAYS 5   Students create original presentations of Civil War events using the software
THROUGH 7   program iMovie.

ASSESSMENT   Develop an assessment rubric that covers the following criteria, adding your own criteria:

Content
- evidence of understanding of Civil War
- collection of images
- appropriate telling of Civil War tale
- storyboarding
- neatness

Technology
- WWW research
- use of graphics editing software
- use of word processor
- use of iMovie

For help in creating rubrics, use as a resource the "Constructing a Rubric" essay found in the Strategies for Getting Started chapter of this book.

Imagination Amusement Park

Students work in small groups to create an Imagination Amusement Park Web site. Each section of the site will offer an amusement park ride or event that celebrates the use of imagination through different student projects developed in this theme. Each event should be interactive and linked to a specific area of the curriculum, much like the theme itself is designed.

O R

Each student selects one of his/her work products and showcases it at a daylong celebration of learning through Imagination. Students can select roles as original characters in costume, storytellers, filmmakers, and Civil War re-enactors, presenting their work to one another in the morning, and then students from other classes can be scheduled in throughout the day to view the amusement park. Parents and the general community can attend too.

Each student should stay in character and provide an interactive experience for interested visitors. Pass out admission tickets and play carnival music for effect and have multimedia presentations on amusement parks and/or amusement park rides playing via television or projector display at a central location for everyone to enjoy.

theme 3

BY SUSAN O'HARA AND MAUREEN MCMAHON

"Where all think alike, no one thinks very much."
—Walter Lippman

Perspectives

Perspective is a fruitful theme for Grades 3–5 as students move into a greater awareness of the world around them. Upper elementary students are developmentally ready to consider other points of view among peers and across cultures. As children begin to make connections beyond their immediate frame of reference, they need to develop a context for receiving new ideas and opinions. Perspective is that evolving context. Through this theme, students will develop a greater understanding of perspective through math, science, social studies, and the arts.

Technology aids in a study of perspective because it breaks down the traditional barriers of time and space. Through use of the Internet, students can conduct research, collaborate with peers, interact with experts and publish their work for others to see. Furthermore, visual digital tools allow students to see and manipulate ideas in ways that the traditional classroom could not offer. Today technology allows students to see many different perspectives in the classrooms regardless of their orientation to learning.

The standards-based lessons in the following curriculum enable students to explore the concept of perspective as they

- create Web-based colonies on different planets;
- write folk tales that come to life with inserted pictures and student drawings;
- make drawings of new colonies to scale using electronic grid or CAD programs;
- interpret paintings from different cultures and different time periods;
- investigate and discuss cultural differences through the use of Internet resources to see the creative uniqueness resident in every culture;
- take digital photographs of their own communities and use them to illustrate their personal folk tales;
- build electronic spreadsheets to better understand the distance of each planet from the sun;
- explore perspective in art through online activities; and
- create their own art masterpieces online at the Museum of Modern Art.

Unit Tools

SPOTLIGHT ON
TECHNOLOGY

Internet Research: One of the most powerful benefits of the Internet in education is that students can have access to real-life, real-time data. In the Perspective in Our World unit, students access the NASA Web site. This allows them to explore real-time data about their planet. It also allows them to see satellite images of the Earth and their community. These experiences are exciting and motivating for the students.

Internet Collaboration: In Perspectives in Cultural Folk Tales, students have an opportunity to talk with peers from around the world. They can access e-mail pen pals from a country of their choice using a Web site such as Intercultural E-mail Classroom Connections (**www.epals.com**). This opportunity for students to connect with their peers from around the world facilitates a deeper appreciation of different cultural perspectives.

Web site Construction: In the Perspective in Art unit, students can create their own works of art, using a Java applet on the Museum of Modern Art Web site. Students can creating art on a Web site where they are also viewing famous works of art from around the world.

Inspiration: Inspiration is a semantic mapping application that allows students to outline, brainstorm, categorize, create hierarchies and show relationships. In this unit Inspiration is used for both the generation of ideas and the planning of projects. Because it is a visual thinking tool, Inspiration can support students who are not typically successful in a text-based environment.

TimeLiner: TimeLiner is another visual tool, helping students to explore time lines, calendars, personal planners and spatial relationships. It is designed especially for upper elementary students and accommodates text, color and graphics. TimeLiner is used in this unit to show graphic representation of distances between planets and to develop student work plans.

CHILDREN'S
LITERATURE

Bunnicula by James Howe
Celebrate America in Poetry and Art by Nora Panzer (editor), National Museum of American Art
The Emperor's New Clothes by Hans Christian Andersen
Frederick by Leo Lionni
How the Devil Got His Cat & Other Multicultural Folktales for Children by Mary Alice Downie
I Am the Cheese by Robert Cormier
Just So Stories by Rudyard Kipling
Little Blue and Little Yellow by Leo Lionni
The Little Prince by Antoine De Saint-Exupéry
The Magic Schoolbus Lost in Space by Joanna Kearns
Maniac Magee by Jerry Spinelli
Me and My Place in Space by Joan Sweeney, illustrated by Annette Cable

TEACHER VOICES
Painting (Behind the Scenes) by Andrew Pekarik
The Prince and the Pauper by Mark Twain
Reading the World with Folktales by Nancy Polette, illustrated by Paul Dillion
Seven Blind Mice by Ed Young
Stone Soup by Marcia Brown
To Space and Back by Sally Ride and Susan Okie
Tuesday by David Wiesner

WRITING ACROSS
THE CURRICULUM

There are many opportunities for integrating writing into these lessons. In the Perspective in Our World unit, students could create a newspaper for their new colony. Teams could write articles, opinion columns, and editorials for the newspaper. In the Perspectives in Cultural Folk Tales, there are numerous writing opportunities, including writing personal folk tales and interpreting folk tales from different cultures around the world. In the Perspective in Art unit, students could create an illustrated report on the history of art or write their own reflections on different paintings of their choice.

TEACHER VOICES

About the Perspective in Our World Unit

"Children are always fascinated by outer space and what worlds exist beyond the planet Earth. In this unit it is exciting to see groups of students explore their own solar system and begin to understand that their world is a smaller part of a larger picture. Through access to images and data from NASA, they begin to compare conditions on Earth with conditions on other planets and develop an understanding of the delicate balance of conditions needed to support human life. The activities and experiences in this unit help students gain a new perspective on the wonders of their planet and the preciousness of life."

About the Perspective in Art Unit

"The interpretation of art is an interesting topic for elementary students. Children explore how different people can interpret the same painting in many different ways. The interpretations are all valid, even though they are not the same. This is an exciting way to have young children begin to discuss the value and importance of multiple perspectives. In this unit, children also explore the concept of perspective in creating art. Through the use of online interactive activities, they get to experience how changing the distances and positions of objects can entirely change a painting."

WEB RESOURCES

Art
African Art: **http://community.middlebury.edu/~atherton/AR325.html**
Early American Paintings: **www.worcesterart.org/Collection/Early_American/**
Gallery: **http://imv.aau.dk/~jfogde/gallery/art/art.html** (Andy Warhol)
Impressionism: **www.impressionism.org/default.htm**

Web Gallery of Art: www.kfki.hu/~arthp/

Cultural Perspective

Cultural Debates Online: http://www.teachtsp2.com/cdonline/
Jaguar's Research Report: http://members.aol.com/tiger8472/science/index.htm
KEO: www.keo.org/uk/pages/default.html (satellite)
Y-press—A Children's News Network: www.ypress.org/default/index.html
You Be the Historian: http://americanhistory.si.edu/hohr/springer/index.htm

Elements

A. Pintura, Art Detective: www.eduweb.com/pintura/
ARTStart: http://albrightknox.org/ArtStart/ASimagesA-I.HTM
Ask Joan of Art: http://nmaa-ryder.si.edu/study/reference-main.html
Sanford Study of Art: www.sanford-artedventures.com/study/study.html

Folk Tales

Absolutely Whootie—Stories to Grow By: www.storiestogrowby.com
Folk Legends of Japan: www.jinjapan.org/kidsweb/folk.html
Folk Tale Project: www.nsc.ru/folk/
Myths, Folk Tales and Fairy Tales:
   http://teacher.scholastic.com/writewit/mff/index.htm
Swahili Folk Tale: http://pbskids.org/africa/tale/index.html

Perspective and Art

Art Safari: http://artsafari.moma.org
Wet Canvas!—Basic Drawing:
   www.wetcanvas.com/ArtSchool/Drawing/BasicDrawing/Lesson2/index.html
Color, Contrast, and Dimension in News Design:
   www.poynter.org/special/colorproject/colorproject/color.html
Drawing in One-Point Perspective: www.olejarz.com/arted/perspective/
Inside Art: www.eduWeb.com/insideart/index.html (Art history)
Learning to Look at Art:
   http://trackstar.hprtec.org/main/track_frames.php3?track_id=22147&nocache
   =9953915
Making a Masterpiece at MoMA:
   http://java.sun.com/features/1999/02/moma.html
A Virtual Tour of Cave Paintings:
   www.harcourtschool.com/activity/cavepaintings/cavepaintings.html

Solar System

Amazing Space: http://amazing-space.stsci.edu/
Astronomy for Kids:
   www.astronomy.com/content/static/AstroForKids/default.asp
BrainPOP—Solar System: www.brainpop.com/science/space/solarsystem/
Exploring Planets in the Classroom:
   www.spacegrant.hawaii.edu/class_acts/index.html
NASA Images: www.nasa.gov/newsinfo/srtm_images.html
Space Physics and Aeronomy Research Collaboratory (SPARC):
   www.windows.ucar.edu/sparc/
A Virtual Journey into the Universe: http://library.thinkquest.org/28327/
Welcome to Our Solar System:
   http://trackstar.hprtec.org/main/track_frames.php3?track_id=64136&nocache
   =1681912339
Welcome to the Planets: http://pds.jpl.nasa.gov/planets/

Writing

Ask a Reporter: www.nytimes.com/learning/students/ask_reporters/

CBBC Newsround: http://news.bbc.co.uk/cbbcnews/
Children's Book Reviews: http://users.erols.com/scholl/
Mike Rophone, the Roving Reporter: www.mikerofone.com/index.html
The Write Site: www.writesite.org

TEACHING TIPS

The most powerful learning environments are those that actively engage the learner and in which students act as both learner and facilitator through sharing their new knowledge.

Most of these lessons will work best if you employ cooperative learning group techniques. Additionally, these lessons are not always designed for all students to do all parts of the lesson. Divide the students into groups and allow the student groups to choose an angle or task that most interests them. What works well is to allow some students to become the "expert" in a specific area and then use an expert-novice mentoring technique. Another important tip is to make connections between what students are learning about different cultures and their own culture and community. Learning is enhanced when students have the opportunity to see how abstract concepts connect to their everyday lives. It is very important to include some reflective discussions after completing the unit and culminating projects. This will allow students to tie all the pieces of the unit together and to develop a deeper understanding of the concept of perspective.

LESSON EXTENDERS

In the Perspective in Our World unit, students could create small advertisements, using iMovie, that outline the benefits of moving to their new colony. This activity can be used to develop an understanding of how powerful messages can be sent through the medium of movies.

Lessons on music and dance interpretation could certainly become a part of any unit on perspectives. Students could investigate the importance of music and dance within different cultures and the many different interpretations of dance and music. Students could also explore interpretation in poetry. They could access poets online and ask them about their interpretation of one of their own poems. A discussion could be held about how the poet's own interpretation compares with the student's interpretation. Illustrated poems could be created by students and given to their peers for interpretation.

Perspective in Our World

In this unit, science, mathematics, and technology are integrated as students explore the solar system. Through team Internet investigations, whole class discussions, multimedia presentations, and online resources used to view their world from space, students begin to view their world from many different perspectives. Mathematics is woven in, as students explore how objects appear smaller at greater distances. Finally, students will gain an understanding of the conditions necessary to support life on Earth and how it compares to the other planets within the solar system.

STANDARDS MET IN THIS UNIT

NETS 2, 3, 5

English Language Arts 1, 3, 7, 8, 12

Math 2, 4, 5

Science A1, A2, B2, D1, D2, D3, F1, F4

Social Studies III h, k

WEB RESOURCES

Solar System
  Amazing Space: http://amazing-space.stsci.edu/
  Astronomy for Kids:
    www.astronomy.com/content/static/AstroForKids/default.asp
  BrainPOP—Solar System: www.brainpop.com/science/space/solarsystem/
  Exploring Planets in the Classroom:
    www.spacegrant.hawaii.edu/class_acts/index.html
  NASA Images: www.nasa.gov/newsinfo/srtm_images.html
  Space Physics and Aeronomy Research Collaboratory (SPARC):
    www.windows.ucar.edu/sparc/
  A Virtual Journey into the Universe: http://library.thinkquest.org/28327/
  Welcome to Our Solar System:
    http://trackstar.hprtec.org/main/track_frames.php3?track_id=6413&nocache
    =1681912339
  Welcome to the Planets: http://pds.jpl.nasa.gov/planets/

SOFTWARE

Inspiration
Microsoft Draw/Paint or Appleworks
Netscape Composer
TimeLiner

DAYS 1 AND 2

In groups of three to four, students brainstorm everything they know about the solar system using Inspiration. They look at celestial bodies for criteria such as size, location, and physical characteristics. Students also discuss how large their world seems. They discuss the size of the sun and moon and why they seem so small in relation to Earth. Students hypothesize about what the Earth would look like from outer space. Having brainstormed the answers to some of these questions, each group shares their ideas with the whole class. As a whole class, students read *The Magic Schoolbus Lost in Space.*

DAYS 3 THROUGH 5

Students complete a Track Star scavenger hunt (use the Welcome to Our Solar System site listed in Web Resources) to familiarize themselves with some of the Internet sites they will be visiting and to facilitate building an understanding of the size of the solar system and how Earth is just one small part. As part of this scavenger hunt, students visit the NASA site, where they can view the Earth and parts of their community from outer space. In teams, students complete the scavenger hunt answering questions about the Earth and the solar system. Students will also gather and enter data on planet distances from the Sun into a spreadsheet and will construct a graph. Students can then enter their data in TimeLiner 4.0 to compare the graphic representation of the distance of the planets in this software application with the graphs they created from their spreadsheets.

DAYS 6 THROUGH 10

Students are given a "space challenge." In their teams they choose a planet to investigate and decide how to develop a colony on this planet. Teams begin this challenge by outlining the information they will need to research on the Internet.

The research should be designed to develop an understanding of the physical characteristics of their planet, how their planet compares to Earth, and the distance of their planet from the Sun. Students construct Venn diagrams in a word processing or draw program, which show similarities and differences between their chosen planet and Earth and what would be different about everyday life on their planet. Teams use a draw program to create a diagram of their colony. Students sketch the housing, transportation, businesses, and other features that will exist on the colony and scan these into the computer. As a culminating project, each team creates a Web-based virtual tour of their colony using Netscape Composer or another HTML editing program. These Web sites include a description of how the colony was designed, illustrated by student diagrams and sketches. When the final Web-based colonies are completed, the class engages in a "round robin" exploration of these virtual colonies, and as a class they discuss the information they learned from visiting each team's colony. Finally, each individual student creates an illustrated story of what life is like on their new planet and how it might be different from Earth.

ASSESSMENT

Develop an assessment rubric that covers the following criteria, adding your own criteria:

Content
- evidence of understanding of the solar system
- Venn diagram
- research
- planet colony
- neatness

Technology
- scavenger hunt
- use of Inspiration
- draw program
- TimeLiner 4.0
- creation of Web site

For help in creating rubrics, use as a resource the "Constructing a Rubric" essay found in the Strategies for Getting Started chapter of this book.

Perspective in Cultural Folk Tales

In this independent study unit, social studies and language arts are woven together as students read a variety of folk tales to develop an appreciation of cultural differences and similarities. Folk tales have been a traditional method of storytelling for centuries. In many cultures, folk tales are a way of explaining nature and behavior. Through this genre, students are able to uncover a piece of another culture, and with it some understanding of different cultural perspectives. Students, in conference with the teacher, will determine the culminating project. It will include a multimedia presentation.

STANDARDS MET IN THIS UNIT

NETS 2, 3, 4, 5, 6
English Language Arts 1–6, 8, 9, 11, 12
Social Studies Ia–e, II

WEB RESOURCES

Folk Tales
  Absolutely Whootie—Stories to Grow By: www.storiestogrowby.com
  Folk Legends of Japan: www.jinjapan.org/kidsweb/folk.html
  Folk Tale Project: www.nsc.ru/folk/
  Myths, Folk Tales and Fairy Tales:
    http://teacher.scholastic.com/writewit/mff/index.htm
  Swahili Folk Tale: http://pbskids.org/africa/tale/index.html

SOFTWARE

HyperStudio
PowerPoint
TimeLiner
Word or Appleworks

DAYS 1 AND 2

After presenting the genre of folk tales, have students read several folk tales. Rudyard Kipling's *Just So Stories* is a great resource. In groups, students will then meet with the teacher to begin an independent study. During this meeting, each group will develop a time line using TimeLiner 4.0 that incorporates meeting times with the teacher and a completion deadline. The teacher will provide students with a list of resources including Web sites. In addition, students will discuss possible project options including:

  ■ Creating an illustrated folk tale (with a different cultural base—looking at dress, food, homes, holidays and ceremonies, agriculture and industry, and animals). This could be created using a word processing program, where students incorporate images from the Internet and personal illustrations that they have scanned into the computer. The illustrated folk tale could also be created in a multimedia program where they can incorporate images and sounds.

- Constructing a map of a country, using it as part of a multimedia presentation along with e-mail communication from someone from that country.

- Preparing a regional dish and an illustrated recipe to accompany the dish, and developing a tutorial of the recipe in a multimedia format.

- Creating a piece of culturally related art and incorporating it into a report on the importance of art in that particular culture.

- Rewriting a folk tale as a play.

DAYS 3 THROUGH 9
Students will work on their independent project. They will be given time to work on classroom computers and in the library to conduct research on the Internet and to use a variety of books. During this time, students will be involved in a variety of activities. Students will e-mail individuals in other countries, scan their own artwork into a computer, take digital photographs of their own community to use in their personal folk tales, and access different folk tales online from a variety of cultures across the world. Each group will then complete its multimedia project, which will be presented to the class.

ASSESSMENT
Develop an assessment rubric that covers the following criteria, adding your own criteria:

Content
- evidence of understanding of the folk tale genre

- ability to create and follow a time line

- individual project

- neatness

- creativity

Technology
- accessing Web resources

- word processor

- TimeLiner 4.0

- multimedia presentation

- scanning

For help in creating rubrics, use as a resource the "Constructing a Rubric" essay found in the Strategies for Getting Started chapter of this book.

Perspective in Art

In this two-week unit, students will explore the use of perspective in art and multiple perspectives about art. They will discuss the importance of art within different cultures and discuss how art has been used to show emotions, display history, and communicate with others. They will develop an understanding for the interpretation of art and discuss how art can be interpreted in many different ways. Students will realize that one of the most important discoveries during the Renaissance was the use of perspective in art. They will explore the meaning of physical perspective through online activities.

STANDARDS MET IN THIS UNIT

NETS 2, 3, 4
English Language Arts 1, 5, 7, 8, 12
Math 3, 4
Social Studies Ia–e, IXa

WEB RESOURCES

Perspective and Art
Art Safari: http://artsafari.moma.org
Wet Canvas!—Basic Drawing:
 www.wetcanvas.com/ArtSchool/Drawing/BasicDrawing/Lesson2/index.html
Color, Contrast, and Dimension in News Design:
 www.poynter.org/special/colorproject/colorproject/color.html
Drawing in One-Point Perspective: www.olejarz.com/arted/perspective/
Inside Art: www.eduWeb.com/insideart/index.html (Art history)
Learning to Look at Art:
 http://trackstar.hprtec.org/main/track_frames.php3?track_id=22147&nocache
 =9953915
Making a Masterpiece at MoMA:
 http://java.sun.com/features/1999/02/moma.html
A Virtual Tour of Cave Paintings:
 www.harcourtschool.com/activity/cavepaintings/cavepaintings.html

SOFTWARE

HyperStudio
PowerPoint

DAYS 1 AND 2

In groups, students discuss what art means to them. They talk about their favorite painting or drawing and why they like it. Each group will examine one painting. They will individually reflect on what the painting means to them. Then they will share their reflections with the rest of the group and discuss how their interpretations were different or similar. A whole class discussion will be held on the different ways people interpret art. In pairs, students will go online and read "Falling into a Painting" at the Inside Art site, and they will take the online quiz that accompanies the story.

DAYS 3 THROUGH 5 Teams of students will conduct a TrackStar Internet scavenger hunt to explore art from different cultures and different time periods in history. They will answer questions about what the paintings reveal about the different cultures and about history. Through this research students will discover that it was during the Renaissance that perspective in art was mastered. Each team will then choose a collection of paintings from online art galleries and write about how perspective was used in these paintings. They will compare early cave paintings with paintings from a later time period and discuss the effect of perspective on art. If time is an issue, teachers might want to preselect sites and even bookmark them for easy access by students.

DAYS 5 THROUGH 9 Each team will create a multimedia presentation that reports on the effect of perspective on art. They will create their own masterpieces online at the Museum of Modern Art and include these in their multimedia presentation.

ASSESSMENT Develop an assessment rubric that covers the following criteria, adding your own criteria:

Content
- evidence of understanding of perspective
- critique of favorite painting
- research
- original artwork
- neatness

Technology
- accessing Web resources
- scavenger hunt
- capturing digital images online and saving them offline
- multimedia presentation

For help in creating rubrics, use as a resource the "Constructing a Rubric" essay found in the Strategies for Getting Started chapter of this book.

Perspective in Writing

In this unit, social studies and language arts are integrated with technology as students examine a variety of writing to develop a sense of point of view and context. After developing an appreciation for perspective in writing, students will be challenged to use a desktop publishing application to create the editorial page of a newspaper from a selected time period in history. Students can build on this learning experience in the final unit of this theme, art criticism.

STANDARDS MET IN THIS UNIT

NETS 2, 3, 4, 5
English Language Arts 1, 4, 5, 7
Social Studies Id, IIa, d, f

WEB RESOURCES

Writing
Ask a Reporter: www.nytimes.com/learning/students/ask_reporters/
CBBC Newsround: http://news.bbc.co.uk/cbbcnews/
Children's Book Reviews: http://users.erols.com/scholl/
Mike Rophone, the Roving Reporter: www.mikerofone.com/index.html
The Write Site: www.writesite.org

Cultural Perspective
Cultural Debates Online: http://www.teachtsp2.com/cdonline/
Jaguar's Research Report: http://members.aol.com/tiger8472/science/index.htm
KEO: www.keo.org/uk/pages/default.html (satellite)
Y-press—A Children's News Network: www.ypress.org/default/index.html
You Be the Historian: http://americanhistory.si.edu/hohr/springer/index.htm

SOFTWARE

Inspiration
Microsoft Draw/Paint or Appleworks
Word or Appleworks

DAY 1

Students participate in Cultural Debates Online (www.teachtsp2.com/cdonline/) in small groups. Each group will focus on appearance, ecotourism, education, land, medicine, or technology. Conclude by sharing findings and discussing how students' perspective affected understanding of the Mentawai tribe.

DAY 2

Have students select and research events from different time periods in history. Each student or small group must collect at least ten facts about the event they have chosen. Once their research is complete, students are asked to create two fictional characters who participated in the historical event. Students can use Inspiration to map out a personality profile of each character: appearance, gender, age, occupation, family and perspective about the event. The two characters should have opposing perspectives about the event: What actually happened or what it actually meant in history?

DAYS 3 AND 4	Using a drawing program, students will create caricatures of both of the fictitious characters they have developed. Both images should be saved in a graphics format that can be imported into a desktop publishing application.
DAYS 5 THROUGH 7	Students will draft editorials written by the two opposing fictitious characters they have created. Both characters will write about the same event from opposing points of view. Both editorials must refer to at least three of the ten facts students gathered in their research. Editorials will be edited, revised and rewritten.
DAYS 8 THROUGH 10	Using a desktop publishing application, students will create a fictional newspaper banner with an editorial header. The document will be split into two columns, one for each editorial piece. Students will then import the original pictures of each fictional writer and their respective editorials, wrapping text around each image.
ASSESSMENT	Develop an assessment rubric that covers the following criteria, adding your own criteria:

Content
- evidence of understanding of point of view
- researching at least ten facts on an historical event
- personality profiles of fictitious characters
- writing, editing, and revising editorials
- neatness

Technology
- participating in online simulation
- use of Inspiration
- use of draw program to create characters
- use of desktop publishing software

For help in creating rubrics, use as a resource the "Constructing a Rubric" essay found in the Strategies for Getting Started chapter of this book.

Perspective in Art Criticism

In this unit, the arts and the language arts come together as students examine a variety of art work and develop the role of being an art critic by referring to elements of art: line, color, shape, perspective and content. The ultimate question each student will answer is "Was this art work successful in accomplishing what it was trying to do?" By backing up their opinion with reference to art elements, students will demonstrate that their perspective is well grounded as art critics.

STANDARDS MET IN THIS UNIT

NETS 2, 3, 4, 5, 6
English Language Arts 1, 3, 6

WEB RESOURCES

Art
    African Art: **http://community.middlebury.edu/~atherton/AR325.html**
    Early American Paintings: **www.worcesterart.org/Collection/Early_American/**
    Gallery: **http://imv.aau.dk/~jfogde/gallery/art/art.html** (Andy Warhol)
    Impressionism: **www.impressionism.org/default.htm**
    Web Gallery of Art: **www.kfki.hu/~arthp/**
Elements
    A. Pintura, Art Detective: **www.eduweb.com/pintura/**
    ARTStart: **http://albrightknox.org/ArtStart/ASimagesA-I.HTM**
    Ask Joan of Art: **http://nmaa-ryder.si.edu/study/reference-main.html**
    Sanford Study of Art: **www.sanford-artedventures.com/study/study.html**

SOFTWARE

Inspiration
PowerPoint

DAY 1

Students participate in the simulation A. Pintura, Art Detective (**www.eduweb.com/pintura/**) in small groups. Each group will work to solve the mystery of the missing painting while analyzing art elements from different schools of painting, all the while keeping notes on art elements, artists and art works. Conclude by using Inspiration to conduct a class brainstorming chart that shows the art elements students are aware of and the different periods of art through history. The web can include artists and examples from each time period as students can recall them.

DAY 2

Have students select and research an artist from a specific school of painting. They must collect at least five digital images of the artist's work and save them locally. The paintings can be around a certain theme or they can be representative of the breadth of the artist's work. In addition to the images, student should gather biographical data (when and where the artist lived, the school of painting the artist is identified with, and a definition of that school's work).

DAYS 3 AND 4   Using a draw program, students will identify the art elements in each image they have captured by highlighting and labeling each element on and around the images. Each labeled image should be saved under a separate name from the original image. For example, monalisa.jpg would be saved as monalisalabel.jpg. In this way, the original images remain untouched.

DAYS 5 AND 6   Students will use the outline mode in PowerPoint to analyze the artist's work. Each bullet will state a specific art element and its definition. Once all pertinent art elements have been bulleted, students will add three bullets on the artist's biographical data and at least five bullets naming each art image they have studied.

DAYS 7 AND 8   Using the slide view and slide sorter view in Power Point, students will add the images on each slide containing a name of a painting done by the artist. They will then add a new slide after each painting slide on which they will insert their labeled image of art elements for each corresponding painting.

DAYS 9 AND 10   Students will share their slide shows with one another. The class will then revisit their Inspiration map of art elements, art and artists and add new learning to the concept map.

ASSESSMENT   Develop an assessment rubric that covers the following criteria, adding your own criteria:

Content
- evidence of understanding of art elements
- research on at least five pieces of art
- collection of biographical data
- critique each piece of art
- neatness

Technology
- participating in online simulation
- use of Inspiration
- capturing digital images online and saving them offline
- manipulation of digital images
- use of PowerPoint

For help in creating rubrics, use as a resource the "Constructing a Rubric" essay found in the Strategies for Getting Started chapter of this book.

Classroom Gallery

Students work in small groups to create a virtual art exhibit Web site. Each section of the site will offer an example of perspective through images of the solar system, folk tales, art and culture, including critiques, opinion pieces and research on each. Each component of the Web site should be interactive and include links to additional Web resources on the theme of perspective.

OR

Each student selects one of his/her work products and showcases it at a daylong celebration of learning through Perspective. Students can select roles as artists, critics, journalists, anthropologists, or astronauts, presenting their work to one another in the morning, and then students from other classes can be scheduled in throughout the day to view the exhibit. Parents and the general community can attend too.

Each student should stay in character and provide an interactive experience for interested visitors. Pass out exhibit programs and have your class wear name tags that include their occupations, and have multimedia presentations on art, culture and the solar system playing via television or projector display at a central location for everyone to enjoy.

theme 4

BY RONI JONES

"Every little movement has a meaning all its own."
——Otto Harbach

Movement

The theme of movement stimulates young minds. Movement represents progress. It suggests a change has occurred. In a world that continues to shrink into that proverbial global village, movement is the metaphor for the state of flux in which we live. No longer is information a static commodity that can be taught in rote chunks. In the Information Age, knowledge is constantly changing and the best we can hope for is to master the tools necessary to keep up with it. For these reasons, movement is a concept students can apply to every area of their studies. It not only provides a framework for information in all its fluid forms, but it presents a context in which students can view the many ways society is evolving in the dawn of the Digital Age.

Technology has unique aspects to help students experience and express the concept of movement. Animated images have become easy to create and the filming and editing of digital movies has opened the door to all kinds of new possibilities for authentic learning tasks and performance assessments. Moreover, digital movement allows students to test new ideas that may not be possible otherwise, due to limitations of money, materials and the classroom environment. Technology can enhance our understanding of movement through its many applications in the classroom.

The standards-based lessons in the following curriculum enable students to use art, math, science, and geography skills to explore concepts of movement across the curriculum. Students will

- design a playground that is universally accessible;

- visualize the movement of agricultural goods to Japan from the United States and the effect of Japan's physical size and features on its inhabitants;

- create an electronic spreadsheet to compare the populations and land areas of Japan and the United States;

- research the natural resources necessary in the manufacture of pencils;

- create a quilt square to represent an important place or event; and

- observe the kinesthetics of movement.

Unit Tools

SPOTLIGHT ON
TECHNOLOGY

Web Publishing: Within these lessons are several areas where technology provides opportunities that may not otherwise exist. For example, in the Movement and Quilting lesson, students are able to submit their quilt designs and stories to a Web site for possible publication. Also, they will develop animated images for a Cyber Circus Web site. The students can then have the experience of developing products for a wider audience.

Draw Program: Lessons in this unit use a draw program to reinforce important concepts and allow students to manipulate images and create a sense of motion. Students will also use a scanner to import copies of images.

Graphics Editing Software: Students will need a graphics editing application in order to crop, resize and manipulate images in this unit. Adobe Photoshop and JASC Paint Shop Pro are two popular packages that not only allow provide for basic image editing, but include the ability to animate images.

Spreadsheet: Spreadsheets are used as a productivity tool that allows students to gather data and use formulae to complete arithmetic operations.

Word Processor: The word processor is used for promoting the writing process and as a desktop publishing tool. Images are imported into the word processor and word processing documents can be transformed into web pages.

CHILDREN'S
LITERATURE

Araminta's Paint Box by Karen Ackerman
Gaijin: Foreign Children in Japan by Olive and Ngaio Hill
Grasshopper Summer by Ann Turner
Heard it in the Playground by Allan Ahlberg
Homecoming by Cynthia Voigt
The Josephina Story Quilt by Eleanor Coerr
The Keeping Quilt by Patricia Polacco
The Log Cabin Quilt by Ellen Howard
Making Pencils by Ruth Thomson
Mysterious Tales of Japan by Rafe Martin
The Patchwork Quilt by Valerie Flourney
Popcorn Days and Buttermilk Nights by Gary Paulsen
Prairie Songs by Pam Conrad
The Quilt Story by Tony Johnson
Sewing Quilts by Ann Turner and Thomas B. Allen
Shizuko's Daughter by Kyoko Mori
Sweet Clara and the Freedom Quilt by Deborah Hopkinson
Turtle Bay by Saviour Pirotta

WRITING ACROSS
THE CURRICULUM

This unit provides several opportunities for students to write across the curriculum. However, there are also other areas in which writing can take place. For example, students have several opportunities to write letters. Students can write friendly letters to students in Japan to discover current fashion and fads. They could also write formal letters to playground companies to order catalogues or request pricing information. Persuasive letters could be written to the local planning commission or school board encouraging safety reviews of current playground. Writing assignments could also be given for students to write creative stories about a trip to Japan or fantasy stories about imaginary playgrounds.

TEACHER VOICES

About the Movement and Math Unit

"While teaching the playground unit, I had many students who were motivated above and beyond the assignments I had given. Many students purchased their own drawing tools and graph paper so that they could work on details of their playground structure. They enjoyed investigating the needs of others who may have limited abilities and making necessary adjustments to their plans so that everyone could have access. I had one student who commented that he had never thought of being an architect until completing the project."

About the Movement and Geography Unit

"After completing the unit on Japan, my students wanted to continue to read books about Japan and to research Web sites about the customs and culture. I had a parent who volunteered to bring in sushi for all of the students to sample. This made the experience of studying Japan come to life."

WEB RESOURCES

Animation
Add Animation and Sounds: www.webgenies.co.uk/add_animation1.htm
GIF Animation Instructions: home.eznet.net/~stevemd/animinst.html
GIFWorks: www.gifworks.com
MediaBuilder 3D Text Maker: www.3dtextmaker.com
VSE Animation Maker: http://vse-online.com/animation-maker/index.html

Body Movement
And They Kept on Dancing: http://library.thinkquest.org/J002266F/
Dancemaker—Paul Taylor: www.dancemaker.org/clips.html
Knowble: www.knowble.com
PE Central Sports Related Sites: http://pe.central.vt.edu/websites/sportsites.html
Turnstep Aerobics: www.turnstep.com

Country Statistics
CIA World Factbook: www.odci.gov/cia/publications/factbook/
Infonation: www.un.org/Pubs/CyberSchoolBus/infonation/e_infonation.htm
Information Please Almanac: http://infoplease.com
Japanese Ministry of Agriculture: www.maff.go.jp/eindex.html
Library of Congress Country Studies: http://memory.loc.gov/frd/cs/cshome.html

Japan
Japan: http://link.lanic.utexas.edu/asnic/countries/japan/
Japan-Guide.com: www.japan-guide.com
Japan, My Japan!: www.lang.nagoya-u.ac.jp/~matsuoka/Japan.html

Japan's Secret Garden: www.pbs.org/wgbh/nova/satoyama/
KidsWeb Japan: http://jin.jcic.or.jp/kidsweb/

Movement
Everest Dispatches:
    www.nationalgeographic.com/everest/dispatches_start22.html
Historic Sites on the Oregon Trail: www.isu.edu/~trinmich/Sites.html
Oregon Trail Diaries: www.isu.edu/~trinmich/00.n.dairies.html
Riding the Overland Stage, 1861: www.ibiscom.com/stage.htm
Schoolhouse Rock, History Rock–Elbow Room:
    www.apocalypse.org/pub/u/gilly/Schoolhouse_Rock/HTML/history/elbow.html

Pencils
Dixon Ticonderoga Company: www.dixonticonderoga.com
General Pencil Company: www.generalpencil.com
Inventing a New Kind of Pencil:
    www.noogenesis.com/inventing/pencil/pencil_page.html
Pencil Pages: www.pencils.com
Shepenco: www.shepenco.com

Playground
Boundless Playgrounds: www.boundlessplaygrounds.org
Kangoroo Playgrounds: www.kangoroo.com
Peaceful Playgrounds: www.peacefulplaygrounds.com
Playland: www.playland-inc.com
Playworld Systems: www.playworldsystems.com

Playground Safety
National Playground Safety Institute: www.opraonline.org/playgrnd/institut.htm
National Program for Playground Safety Report Cards:
    www.uni.edu/playground/report.html
Playground Safety:
    www.kidsource.com/kidsource/content5/playground.safety.sb1a.html
Playground Safety Publications: www.cpsc.gov/cpscpub/pubs/playpubs.html

Quilts
Amish Quilts from Lancaster County:
    http://206.204.3.133/dir_nii/nii_esprit.html
PBS Quilts–Classroom: http://pbs.org/americaquilts/classroom/index.html
Quilt Art: www.miamisci.org/hurricane/quiltart.html
Quilts and Quiltmaking in America (1978–1996):
    http://memory.loc.gov/ammem/qlthtml/qlthome.html
Quilts over Kosovo: http://globaldevelopment.org/quilterinfo.htm

Reflective Writing
Diary of a Park Ranger: www.dnr.state.wi.us/org/caer/ce/eek/job/ranger.htm
KidsHealth–My Journal: http://kidshealth.org/misc_pages/journal/index.html
A Soldier's Diary: www.ukans.edu/carrie/kancoll/articles/cruzan/index.html
The Write Site–Style Section: www.writesite.org/html/style.html

TEACHING TIPS   All of these units work best if students have some experience with Internet research and multimedia programs. As students progress through these units, they will gain experience in applying the programs to solve problems and create products for a variety of audiences. In most of the activities, cooperative groups could be employed to support learners who need more assistance in the use of technology. Student technology mentors can be appointed to answer questions and help students to become more self-directed and self-reliant.

LESSON EXTENDERS

In the unit on Japan, students can extend their learning by investigating cultural aspects of Japan. They can visit sites to discover information about food, music, traditional dress, or religion.

In the unit on quilting, students can research more facts about slavery and the underground railroad. Students could create quilt maps of their own about their local town or neighborhood.

In the unit on playground design, students can extend their learning by doing more research about playground safety. Specific Web sites and ideas are listed at the end of the unit.

In the unit on pencil manufacturing, students can extend their learning by doing research about the use of other natural resources, such as water, copper, or coal. Students can find out how these resources are used and how manufacturers are working to preserve them.

Movement and Geography

In this unit, students will study the ties that bind America's agricultural community to Japan. They will understand the growing level of interdependence between nations in today's globalized society. Students use graphics programs to chart the flow of goods between nations and to understand the relative size and population densities of various nations.

STANDARDS MET IN THIS UNIT

NETS 1, 2, 3, 4, 5, 6
English Language Arts 1, 3, 5, 7
Math 4, 5
Social Studies IIIa, c, g, h; VIIb, h

WEB RESOURCES

Country Statistics
 CIA World Factbook: www.odci.gov/cia/publications/factbook/
 Infonation: www.un.org/Pubs/CyberSchoolBus/infonation/e_infonation.htm
 Information Please Almanac: http://infoplease.com
 Japanese Ministry of Agriculture: www.maff.go.jp/eindex.html
 Library of Congress Country Studies: http://memory.loc.gov/frd/cs/cshome.html

Japan
 Japan: http://link.lanic.utexas.edu/asnic/countries/japan/
 Japan-Guide.com: www.japan-guide.com
 Japan, My Japan!: www.lang.nagoya-u.ac.jp/~matsuoka/Japan.html
 Japan's Secret Garden: www.pbs.org/wgbh/nova/satoyama/
 KidsWeb Japan: http://jin.jcic.or.jp/kidsweb/

SOFTWARE

Excel or Appleworks
Microsoft Draw/Paint or Appleworks
Word or Appleworks

DAYS 1 AND 2

Students research the interdependence between United States and Japanese agriculture. Using the scanner, clip art, or Web images, have students create a collage of agricultural products imported by Japan from the United States. Once printed, these images can be cut into the shape of the United States or Japan. Collages can then be mounted on a bulletin board. As students are creating these images, they can discuss why so much food is moved from the United States to Japan.

DAY 3

Students will research the current populations and land areas of Japan and the United States. Teachers who feel comfortable allowing their students to conduct Internet searches can explain search techniques using keywords such as "almanac," "Japan," or the "United States". If time is an issue, teachers might want to preselect a site and even bookmark it for easy access by students. A suggested site for this information is **http://infoplease.com**. If Internet access is not available, this information can be found in any almanac.

DAY 4 Using the data collected, students can create a spreadsheet to calculate the population density of Japan and the United States. Population density is the total population divided by the total land area. Once the population density is known, comparisons can be drawn about the living conditions in each place. While Japan is 1/25 the size of the United States, it has half as many people as the United States. This means that Japan is very crowded and lacks adequate space to grow its own food. In small groups, have students brainstorm a list of possible problems associated with a high population density.

DAYS 5 AND 6 To create a concrete understanding of what high population density looks like, students will create a pictorial representation using the draw program. Have the students draw a 25 x 25 cm square to represent the size of the United States. Within this square, students will need to place 27 circles (1 cm in diameter) to represent the population of the United States. Encourage the students to spread out these circles to cover as much of the available space as possible. Discuss what it would be like to live in a place where the population density is similar to the one represented in the 25 x 25 cm square.

On a second page, have students create a square 5 x 5 cm. The smaller square represents the size of Japan. Within this square, have students place 13 circles (1 cm in diameter) to represent the population of Japan. Discuss what it would be like to live in a place where the population density is similar to the one represented in the 5 x 5 cm square. The food grown in Japan can sustain only 42% of the population. Fill in five circles with red to represent food grown in Japan. Food grown in the United States sustains 30% of Japan's population. Fill in four circles with yellow to represent food grown in the United States. Food grown in other countries sustains 28% of the population. Fill in the remaining four circles with green to represent food grown in other countries. Because Japan is so mountainous, only one-third of the country is inhabitable. Move all of the circles to fill only one-third of the square to truly represent the population density in Japan. Print out these pictorial representations of Japan's population density and its origin of food supply.

DAY 7 Reviewing the pictorial representation of population density and food origin in Japan, have the students work in pairs or triads to write a short essay using a word processor to explain Japan's dependence on the United States' agriculture and the movement of goods from one country to the other. Students should also compare the living space available in Japan and the United States and its consequences on living conditions.

ASSESSMENT Develop an assessment rubric that covers the following criteria, adding your own criteria:

Content
- agriculture collage

- research

- evidence of understanding of agricultural interdependence

- evidence of understanding of population density

- neatness

Technology
- use of drawing program

- use of spreadsheet

- use of formulae

- use of word processor

For help in creating rubrics, use as a resource the "Constructing a Rubric" essay found in the Strategies for Getting Started chapter of this book.

Movement and Art

In this unit, students will develop an understanding of quilts as a medium to preserve history and culture. They will use graphics programs to study the patterns associated with quilting and produce their own quilt squares.

STANDARDS MET IN THIS UNIT

NETS 1, 2, 3, 4, 5
English Language Arts 1, 2, 5, 6, 7, 8, 11
Social Studies Ia, c; IIc; VId, f

WEB RESOURCES

Quilts
   Amish Quilts from Lancaster County:
      http://206.204.3.133/dir_nii/nii_esprit.html
   PBS Quilts—Classroom: http://pbs.org/americaquilts/classroom/index.html
   Quilt Art: www.miamisci.org/hurricane/quiltart.html
   Quilts and Quiltmaking in America (1978–1996):
      http://memory.loc.gov/ammem/qlthtml/qlthome.html
   Quilts over Kosovo: http://globaldevelopment.org/quilterinfo.htm

SOFTWARE

Microsoft Draw/Paint or Appleworks
Word or Appleworks

DAYS 1 AND 2

In many children's stories, quilts have been an important source to move culture and history through generations. In *Sweet Clara and the Freedom Quilt* by Deborah Hopkinson and illustrated by James Ransome, the slave girl Clara creates a quilt that will guide runaway slaves to the Underground Railroad. This quilt is not only a map, but also shows all the places within her world on the plantation and the story of other slaves in their journey to freedom. Teachers who feel comfortable allowing their students to conduct Internet searches can explain search techniques using keywords such as "quilting" or "quilts". If time is an issue, teachers might want to bookmark a site for easy access by students. Some suggested Web sites are:

   Quilt Art: www.miamisci.org/hurricane/quiltart.html (Reactions to Hurricane Andrew)
   Quilts over Kosovo: http://globaldevelopment.org/quilterinfo.htm (Stories of quilts sent to Kosovo to help refugees)

DAYS 3 THROUGH 5

Examine modern quilt patterns. Teachers who feel comfortable allowing their students to conduct Internet searches can explain search techniques using keywords such as "modern quilts". If time is an issue, teachers might want to preselect a site and even bookmark it for easy access by students. Some suggested Web sites are:

   Amish Quilts from Lancaster County:
      http://206.204.3.133/dir_nii/nii_esprit.html (Revere Collection)

Quilts and Quiltmaking in America (1978–1996):
http://memory.loc.gov/ammem/qlthtml/qlthome.html (American Folklife Center at the Library of Congress)

Have students save a favorite quilt pattern and import it into a draw program. Students can then label the quilt with elements such as line, color, shape, pattern, picture, and any theme created. This labeled image can then be saved in a student portfolio. Using the same draw program with a grid of one-inch squares, students can begin to design their own quilts. Ask students to choose a location or an event that is important to them. The quilt square should be an abstract representation of how this event or location makes them feel.

DAYS 6 AND 7 Have students visit the PBS Quilt site at **http://pbs.org/americaquilts/classroom**. At this site, students can view quilt squares created by artists and read the stories behind the quilt squares by clicking on Meet the Quilters. Students will be asked to reflect on the story their own quilts tell, and how it would be presented on the Meet the Quilters Web page. Using a word processor, students will then tell the story of their quilt. This can be in the form of an essay or a poem. Each student quilt can be imported into the word processing document containing its story. Stories can then be printed and assembled in a book to accompany the quilt as it moves through the grade level or through the school. The movement of these stories is important to the heritage of the students and the classroom. The digital collection of student work can be posted on the class or school Web site. Additionally, directions for submitting the quilt squares and stories are available at the PBS Quilts Web site by clicking on Online Gallery.

ASSESSMENT Develop an assessment rubric that covers the following criteria, adding your own criteria:

Content
- evidence of understanding of quilt storytelling and design elements
- original quilt design
- quilt story
- accuracy of research
- ability to draw conclusions from data
- creativity

Technology
- use of scanner
- saving and importing Web-based images
- use of drawing program
- use of word processor

For help in creating rubrics, use as a resource the "Constructing a Rubric" essay found in the Strategies for Getting Started chapter of this book.

Movement and Math

In this unit, students work in cooperative groups to design the ideal playground. Students observe, classify, and record typical playground activities, and then research playground construction techniques. Students learn important concepts of scale.

STANDARDS MET IN THIS UNIT

NETS 1, 2, 3, 5, 6
English Language Arts 1, 4
Math 3, 4, 5, 6, 7, 8

WEB RESOURCES

Playground
Boundless Playgrounds: www.boundlessplaygrounds.org
Kangoroo Playgrounds: www.kangoroo.com
Peaceful Playgrounds: www.peacefulplaygrounds.com
Playland: www.playland-inc.com
Playworld Systems: www.playworldsystems.com

Playground Safety
National Playground Safety Institute: www.opraonline.org/playgrnd/institut.htm
National Program for Playground Safety Report Cards:
    www.uni.edu/playground/report.html
Playground Safety:
    www.kidsource.com/kidsource/content5/playground.safety.sb1a.html
Playground Safety Publications: www.cpsc.gov/cpscpub/pubs/playpubs.html

SOFTWARE

Excel or Appleworks
HyperStudio
Microsoft Draw/Paint or Appleworks
PowerPoint
Word or Appleworks

DAYS 1 AND 2

Divide students into cooperative groups of four to five. The students will act as a team to observe the movement and activities on an elementary playground. Students will record the movements of the students. Teams may also use a digital camera to capture examples of different kinds of movement. These movements include climbing, crawling, jumping, running, walking, skipping, sitting, standing, and talking. Encourage the students to be specific in their choice of words. "Playing" could be any number of activities. Once the students have created a list of movement words, they will need to use a spreadsheet program to create a record sheet listing these activities. Once students have printed these record sheets, they will tally the movements most observed within a regular recess period on the playground. This record sheet will be the basis for students designing a playground that promotes these activities.

DAYS 3 AND 4 Teachers who feel comfortable allowing their students to conduct Internet searches can explain search techniques using keywords such as "pencil." If time is an issue, teachers might want to preselect a site and bookmark it for easy access by students. Students should be looking for information about making playgrounds and structures accessible to all children regardless of physical handicap. Some suggested Web sites are:

Boundless Playgrounds: www.**boundlessplaygrounds.org** (a nonprofit organization dedicated to helping communities throughout the world create universally accessible playgrounds for their children)

Playground Equipment Manufacturers
www.kangoroo.com
www.playland-inc.com
www.playworldsystems.com

If students visit Boundless Playgrounds first, they will be able to read about issues related to making all playground accessible to all children. When they visit other commercial sites, they can then evaluate the accessibility of the equipment offered. At the commercial sites, students will also need to look for the "bird's eye view" drawings of the playground structures. These will serve as examples for the next part of the activity. Once their research is complete, students will use a draw program to create the layout for a proposed playground. Students should take into account the need for ramps and walkways wide enough to accommodate wheelchairs and alternate activities for children who may not be able to climb or swing.

DAYS 5 THROUGH 8 Students can work in small groups with pattern blocks to begin designing individual play structures. Once a piece of equipment has been designed, students can use a draw program to create a "bird's eye view" of the equipment. Students will need to design their structure with ratio and proportion in mind. The climbing ladder and slide need to be in proportion to the bridge and walkway. On the final printed copy, students should include a scale (1/4 inch = 1 foot). The teacher could even try to get an architect to do a guest presentation in the classroom about the use of technology in design and engineering.

Once the playground layout and individual pieces of equipment have been designed, each small group can design an individual card or slide in a multimedia application that showcases the group's newly designed piece of equipment and explains its size, functionality, and safety features. A separate small group can design a card or slide that maps the layout of the entire proposed playground. Once all cards/slides are completed, each image of playground equipment on the layout can be linked to the individual presentations of specific equipment to form an interactive, multimedia presentation. Students may add sound clips of their voices describing their ideas.

EXTENSION Students can use a spreadsheet to create a budget based on the cost of commercial structures.

Student can do research about playground safety at these suggested Web sites:

www.cpsc.gov/cpscpub/pubs/playpubs.html
www.kidsource.com/kidsource/content5/playground.safety.sb1a.html
www.opraonline.org/playgrnd/institut.htm
www.uni.edu/playground/report.html

ASSESSMENT Develop an assessment rubric that covers the following criteria, adding your own criteria:

Content
- research
- evidence of playground design considerations
- evidence of playground safety considerations
- original equipment design
- neatness

Technology
- use of spreadsheet
- access of Web resources
- use of drawing program
- use of multimedia application

For help in creating rubrics, use as a resource the "Constructing a Rubric" essay found in the Strategies for Getting Started chapter of this book.

Movement and Science

In this unit, students use research skills to explore the use of natural resources—as a scientific, cultural, and economic concept. Students study the process of how companies start with trees and end up with pencils.

STANDARDS MET IN THIS UNIT	NETS 1, 2, 3, 4, 5
	English Language Arts 5, 6, 8
	Science E3, F3, F4

WEB RESOURCES

Pencils

Dixon Ticonderoga Company: www.dixonticonderoga.com
General Pencil Company: www.generalpencil.com
Inventing a New Kind of Pencil:
   www.noogenesis.com/inventing/pencil/pencil_page.html
Pencil Pages!: www.pencils.com
Shepenco: www.shepenco.com

SOFTWARE

HyperStudio
Inspiration
Microsoft Draw/Paint or Appleworks
PowerPoint
Word or Appleworks

DAYS 1 AND 2

The use of natural resources is an important science concept. One everyday object that all students need is the wooden pencil. The teacher can read *Making Pencils* by Ruth Thomson, to familiarize the students with the process of creating Cumberland art pencils in Keswick, Great Britain. From the information in the story, students can use Inspiration to create a graphic organizer that shows the steps in pencil production.

DAYS 3 AND 4

Teachers who feel comfortable allowing their students to conduct Internet searches can explain search techniques using keywords such as "pencils". If time is an issue, teachers might want to preselect a site and even bookmark it for easy access by students. Students should be looking for information about manufacturing pencils. Some possible sites are:

Pencil Pages!: www.pencils.com (Incense Cedar Institute)
General Pencil Company: www.generalpencil.com
Shepenco: www.shepenco.com
Dixon Ticonderoga Company: www.dixonticonderoga.com

The Incense Cedar Institute site offers students the opportunity to explore topics such as pencil history, pencil making, and pencil trivia. Students can practice copying and pasting information from the Web sites into a word processing document. These notes can be printed out and saved for use in later activities.

DAYS 5 AND 6   The Cumberland Pencil Company moves natural resources from all over the world to manufacture the pencils. Students can use the information from *Making Pencils* to list the necessary natural resources and the sources of these natural resources. Some of the natural resources include incense cedar from California; chalk from France; clay and color pigments from Great Britain and Germany; wax from Brazil, the Czech Republic, and Japan; and gum from Iraq and Iran. In cooperative groups, students can research countries from which these materials are imported and report this information back to the class in the form of a multimedia presentation.

DAYS 7 AND 8   Students can work in pairs to email the Incense Cedar Institute at www.pencils.com. The institute provides informational packets, brochures, and posters about the process of pencil manufacturing and the use of incense cedar from California. Students can use a draw and paint program to create an illustration for the institute's annual calendar contest while visiting the Web site.

DAYS 9 AND 10   Students can use the information gained from *Making Pencils*, Internet research, and packets from the Incense Cedar Institute to create a bingo card in a spreadsheet program. They can include facts, vocabulary, and trivia to fill in the squares. Once the cards are printed, the entire class can have fun enjoying a unique game of bingo.

DAYS 11 AND 12   All of the natural resources used in the manufacture of pencils are renewable resources if managed responsibly. Students can do some research about renewable resources on the Internet. Teachers who feel comfortable allowing their students to conduct Internet searches can explain search techniques using keywords such as "pencils". If time is an issue, teachers might want to preselect a site and even bookmark it for easy access by students. Students should be looking for information about manufacturing pencils. From the information gathered, students can work in pairs or triads to write persuasive letters to the Cumberland Pencil factory, the Incense Cedar Institute, or any other company to advocate responsible management of natural resources.

ASSESSMENT   Develop an assessment rubric that covers the following criteria, adding your own criteria:

Content
- research
- persuasive letter format
- persuasive letter content
- understanding of natural resource management
- neatness
- grammar

Technology
- access of Web resources

- use of draw program

- use of spreadsheet

- use of word processor

For help in creating rubrics, use as a resource the "Constructing a Rubric" essay found in the Strategies for Getting Started chapter of this book.

Movement and Writing

In this unit, students use journal writing to explore how movement is communicated. Students will explore different journals to gain an understanding of movement in the human experience. By applying their understanding of movement to journal writing, students will create original writing that shares personal experiences of movement in life.

STANDARDS MET IN THIS UNIT	NETS 2, 3, 4, 5, 6 English Language Arts 2, 3, 4, 7

WEB RESOURCES

Movement
Everest Dispatches:
    www.nationalgeographic.com/everest/dispatches_start22.html
Historic Sites on the Oregon Trail: www.isu.edu/~trinmich/Sites.html
Oregon Trail Diaries: www.isu.edu/~trinmich/00.n.dairies.html
Riding the Overland Stage, 1861: www.ibiscom.com/stage.htm
Schoolhouse Rock, History Rock–Elbow Room:
    www.apocalypse.org/pub/u/gilly/Schoolhouse_Rock/HTML/history/elbow.html

Reflective Writing
And They Kept on Dancing: http://library.thinkquest.org/J002266F/
Diary of a Park Ranger: www.dnr.state.wi.us/org/caer/ce/eek/job/ranger.htm
KidsHealth–My Journal: http://kidshealth.org/misc_pages/journal/index.html
A Soldier's Diary: www.ukans.edu/carrie/kancoll/articles/cruzan/index.html
The Write Site–Style Section: www.writesite.org/html/style.html

SOFTWARE

HyperStudio
Inspiration
Microsoft Draw/Paint or Appleworks
PowerPoint
Word or Appleworks

DAY 1

Students read Mark Twain's reflection on Riding the Overland Stage (www.ibiscom.com/stage.htm) and note the kinds of movement that take place. The class will then discuss who Twain's audience was. Was he writing for himself? In what tense is the reflection written? What do we learn about Twain from this piece of writing? Use Inspiration to brainstorm everything students know about Mark Twain from reading his reflection.

DAY 2

Students read The Write Site–Style Section (www.writesite.org/html/style.html). Discuss how writing for oneself is different from writing for an audience. Set up individual floppy disks or password protected network logins for each student where students can save daily journal entries. Have students enter their first journal entries and save to disk.

DAY 3 Students read Diary of a Park Ranger (**www.dnr.state.wi.us/org/caer/ce/eek/job/ ranger.htm**) and consider the role of observation in journal writing. Have students take a tour of the school grounds with notebooks and digital cameras and take notes on their surroundings. Once students return to the room, they write diary entries using a word processor and import any images they captured with their digital cameras.

DAYS 4 AND 5 Students can choose to read A Soldier's Diary (**www.ukans.edu/carrie/kancoll/ articles/cruzan/index.html**), KidsHealth—My Journal, (**http://kidshealth.org/ misc_pages/journal/index.html**) or And They Kept on Dancing (**http://library. thinkquest.org/J002266F/**). After exploring their selected sites, students will compose a journal entry based on their reading. Entries may include new material learned, questions unanswered, and personal experiences relating to the topic. Save entries to disk.

DAYS 6 AND 7 Students study the Oregon Trail Diaries (**www.isu.edu/~trinmich/00.n.dairies.html**) and copy and paste passages into their digital journals that reveal something about the journal writers. Students will then examine Historic Sites on the Oregon Trail (**www.isu.edu/~trinmich/Sites.html**) and select two stopping points to read about. Based on their reading of primary source diaries, students will type their own fictitious journal entries about travel along that portion of the trail. Fictional entries should be in the first person and reveal elements of the "writer's" character in the way events are revealed. Students may also create original digital images to import into their entries.

DAYS 8 THROUGH 10 As a culminating project, students will share their journal entries with the class. The entries will then be compiled into one common folder where they can be transformed into a multimedia presentation or a Web page.

ASSESSMENT Develop an assessment rubric that covers the following criteria, adding your own criteria:

Content
- evidence of understanding of author's voice in the first person
- journal writing
- fictional journal entries
- neatness
- creativity

Technology
- accessing Web-based resources
- use of Inspiration
- use of a draw program

- use of a word processor
- creation of multimedia presentation or Web page

For help in creating rubrics, use as a resource the "Constructing a Rubric" essay found in the Strategies for Getting Started chapter of this book.

Movement and the Body

In this unit, students not only learn about body movement, but actually learn how to animate pictures to show movement. Applying their understanding of movement to dance and animation, students will make use of digital cameras and graphic editing software in order to create their own original animated graphics, which can be included in multimedia presentations.

STANDARDS MET IN THIS UNIT	NETS 2, 3, 4, 5, 6 English Language Arts 1

WEB RESOURCES

Animation
Add Animation and Sounds: www.webgenies.co.uk/add_animation1.htm
GIF Animation Instructions: home.eznet.net/~stevemd/animinst.html
GIFWorks: www.gifworks.com
MediaBuilder 3D Text Maker: www.3dtextmaker.com
VSE Animation Maker: http://vse-online.com/animation-maker/index.html

Body Movement
And They Kept on Dancing: http://library.thinkquest.org/J002266F/
Dancemaker—Paul Taylor: www.dancemaker.org/clips.html
Knowble: www.knowble.com
PE Central Sports Related Sites: http://pe.central.vt.edu/websites/sportsites.html
Turnstep Aerobics: www.turnstep.com

SOFTWARE

Adobe Photoshop
Netscape Composer
Paint Shop Pro (with Animation Shop)

DAY 1

Students study movement Web sites listed above and explore different body movements in slow motion through dance, exercise, individual athletics and sports. Teacher takes digital pictures of students in different stages of movement. Ideally picture will be taken in two stages in quick succession of one another. Each student will be given his or her own floppy disk with at least 2 (or more) digital images of them experimenting with body movement. Students can view their images using Adobe Photoshop, Paint Shop Pro, or whatever other graphics editor you may have. Images should be converted to .GIF format.

DAY 2

Students read tutorials on how to make animations found at www.webgenies.co.uk/add_animation1.htm and home.eznet.net/~stevemd/animinst.html. Using a projector at the front of the class, teachers will demonstrate how to crop images and then place them in animation frames. Students will practice cropping and animating images using graphic editing software.

DAYS 3 THROUGH 5 Students in small groups take additional pictures of one another and practice manipulating them to create single animated images.

DAYS 6 THROUGH 8 Students in small groups create animated images on dance and circus themes. They may choose to wear costumes and take photographs or create original drawings that can be animated.

DAYS 9 AND 10 Students in small groups will complete a Web page showing off their animated images.

ASSESSMENT Develop an assessment rubric that covers the following criteria, adding your own criteria:

Content
- evidence of understanding of body movement
- evidence of understanding of how to show movement
- developing images on a topic
- neatness
- creativity

Technology
- use of digital camera
- use of graphic editing software
- use of Web resources
- development of Web site

For help in creating rubrics, use as a resource the "Constructing a Rubric" essay found in the Strategies for Getting Started chapter of this book.

Cyber Circus

Students work in small groups to create a Cyber Circus Web site. Like a multi-ring circus, each section of the site will offer a different example of student work illustrating movement through dance, playgrounds, quilts, journals and cultural exchange. Each component of the Web site should be interactive and include links to additional Web resources on the theme of movement.

OR

Each student selects one of his/her work products and showcases it at a daylong celebration of learning through Movement. Students can select roles as writers, performers, quilters and Japanese artists, presenting their work to one another in the morning, and then students from other classes can be scheduled in throughout the day to view the exhibit. Parents and the general community can attend, too.

Each student should stay in character and provide an interactive experience for interested visitors. Have a center ring where events can be announced and multimedia presentations can be shown for effect.

"Change is upsetting.
Repetition is tedious. Three
cheers for variation!"

—Mason Cooley

BY RONI JONES, SUSAN O'HARA, AND HEATHER HOFFMAN

Change

Children can observe change all around them, and in this sense change is a great theme for sharpening students' skills of observation. Change occurs in nature, in our communities, and throughout history. Coming to a deeper understanding of the concept of change helps students in every area of the curriculum, because in every area of education, growth and progress is measured by change. Change not only helps us filter what has already happened, but gives us the perspective to be able to predict what is yet to come. In this sense, it ties in all of the preceding themes in this book. And because change happens over time, many of the units contained herein are designed to last the length of a school year, rather than over the span of days or weeks.

Technology is perhaps the greatest symbol of change in our world today. Just one hundred years ago, many of the technologies we take for granted today didn't exist. These technologies have improved our quality of life and our ability to appreciate the possibilities for even more advances in the future. In this theme technology is used to document and appreciate how change takes place around us in the classroom, the community, and our nation.

The standards-based lessons in the following curriculum enable students to explore the concepts of change as they

- create and maintain spreadsheets to track change in height;
- develop multimedia presentations about change in their school and community;
- import digital photos to multimedia presentations to show change;
- investigate and research change in the life cycle and migration patterns of the monarch butterfly; and
- write stories that come to life with inserted pictures and student artwork.

Unit Tools

SPOTLIGHT ON
TECHNOLOGY

Statistical Software: Students have the opportunity to use statistical software to organize, interpret, and present data they collect about their personal growth and change in their school and community.

Creating Multimedia Presentations: Students can use multimedia tools such as PowerPoint or HyperStudio to present their graphs and data about personal growth and the change in their school and community over time. They can even import digital movies as part of a larger presentation. PowerPoint has the added Web page feature, allowing students to transform their presentations into an online culminating event at the end of the theme.

Internet Research: Students will be able to use the Internet to research the migration patterns of monarch butterflies. This research will allow students to create their own migration maps, which can then be scanned in for their multimedia presentations. Students will also use the Internet to research climate changes and women's history.

Creating and Editing Digital Photos: Digital cameras and photo-editing software are used to record students' changes in height and changes in fauna growth around their school.

Digital Semantic Mapping: Use of a semantic mapping tool such as Inspiration allows students the chance to generate a variety of ideas through its Rapid Fire function or to visually arrange and sort ideas into different categories and hierarchies. Inspiration also allows them to import images and use links to create a more vibrant and interactive sharing of ideas. Inspiration maps can be saved as digital images and then presented in Web pages.

CHILDREN'S LITERATURE

The Big Butterfly Book by Susan Santoro Whayne, illustrated by Rosalinda Solomon
Borning Room by Paul Fleischman
The Butterfly by Sabrina Crewe
Constance: a Story of Early Plymouth by Patricia Clapp
Gotta Go! Gotta Go! by Sam Sworpe
Don't You Know There's a War On by James Stevenson
Letting Swift River Go by Jane Yolen and Barbara
Looking Back: A Book of Memories by Lois Lowry
Monarch Butterfly by Gail Gibbons
Monarch Butterfly's Life by John Himmelman
The Moon and I by Betsy Byars
A River Ran Wild: An Environmental History by Lynne Cherry
Through the Lock by Carol Otis Hurst

WRITING ACROSS THE CURRICULUM

Within this unit are several opportunities for students to write across the curriculum. However, there are also other areas in which writing can take place. Within the Change and Me unit, students can keep a journal of personal, school, and community changes; write poems about feelings associated with change; and write a letter thanking the individual who was interviewed. Within the Change and Science unit, students can write butterfly stories, persuasive essays to set aside land for butterfly migration, haikus with facts about butterflies, and technical explanations of metamorphosis.

TEACHER VOICES   About the Change and Me Unit

"Children love to measure their own growth. The Change and Me unit allows students to go beyond just measuring themselves every month. With this unit they get to create charts and a picture portfolio to chart their progress. It makes for a great end-of-the-year project."

About the Change and Science Unit

"I think all kids at some time have watched a cocoon turn into a butterfly. But then what? Most of the really interesting story is missed. However, with the Change and Science unit, students get to keep track of the butterflies after the metamorphosis. Using the Internet and Inspiration software, students monitor the progress of the butterflies as they migrate across the country."

WEB RESOURCES   **Butterflies**
Children's Butterfly Site: www.mesc.nbs.gov/butterfly/Butterfly.html
Journey North: www.learner.org/jnorth/
Milkweed Café: www.milkweedcafe.com/
Monarch Butterflies: www.pacificgrove.com/butterflies/index.html
Monarch Watch: www.monarchwatch.org/
Sharon's Monarch Butterfly Site: http://home.wi.rr.com/monarchraising/

Community
Build a Community:
    www.pbs.org/klru/forgottenamericans/buildcomm/community.htm
Hometown Heroes: www.weta.org/productions/hheroes/
Italian-American Traditions:
    www.balchinstitute.org/museum/italian/italian2.html
Kids and Community: www.planning.org/kidsandcommunity/
What Kids Can Do: www.whatkidscando.org/intro.html

Growth
Are You Taller in the Morning?:
    www.shu.ac.uk/schools/sci/sol/invest/height/height.htm
BodyQuest: http://library.thinkquest.org/10348/
BrainPOP—Growth and Genetics:
    www.brainpop.com/health/growthanddevelopment/
Flintstones Growth Chart: www.flintstonesvitamins.ca/kids/growth/home.html
Growth Chart: www.chennaikids.com/growthchart/growthchart.shtml

Minorities
"Jim Crow" America: www.ushmm.org/olympics/zcc036a.htm
Powerful Days: www.civilrightsphotos.com/Pages/index2.html
Stand Up for Your Rights: www.pbs.org/wgbh/amex/kids/civilrights/
Time Line of the American Civil Rights Movement:
    www.wmich.edu/politics/mlk/

Seasons
BrainPOP—Seasons: www.brainpop.com/science/weather/seasons/index.weml
Four Seasons @ the Farm: www.redbudfarms.com/hist.four.seasons.htm
New Science—A Change of Seasons:
    http://liftoff.msfc.nasa.gov/news/2001/news-autumnalequinox.asp

New Science—The First Day of Spring:
   http://kids.msfc.nasa.gov/News/2000/News-VernalEquinox.asp
The Wonderful World of Trees: www.domtar.com/arbre/english/start.htm

Women
Military Women Veterans: http://userpages.aug.com/captbarb/
History of Women's Suffrage: www.rochester.edu/SBA/history.html
Not for Ourselves Alone: www.pbs.org/stantonanthony/
Time for Kids—Women's History Month:
   www.timeforkids.com/TFK/specials/0,6709,101044,00.html
Woman's Suffrage and the 19th Amendment:
   www.nara.gov/education/teaching/woman/home.html

TEACHING TIPS

Before the unit begins, the teacher may want to ask critical questions about the concept of change and how it relates to the students' own experiences. In this unit, many of the lessons will work best if cooperative learning techniques are employed. Divide the students into groups and allow student groups to choose a task or concept that most interests them. Once research is completed, students can act as experts on their research topics and assist other groups in gathering important information. After presentations, the teachers should lead a reflective discussion to tie in all activities and synthesize information to reinforce the concept of change.

LESSON EXTENDERS

This unit can be extended through the use of a variety of children's literature. Additionally, pen pals in areas of butterfly migration can be found through www.epals.com. Students can exchange any of their writing, stories, or scanned materials about themselves, their school, their community, or the monarch butterfly. Monarch butterflies can be created using tissue paper, papier-mâché, or a variety of art mediums. Digital pictures of the artwork can then be used with multimedia or e-pals. Live caterpillars can be purchased and raised through sites such as the Mentor Mercantile Company at www.mentormerc.com/mentormerc/butladandmor.html.

Change and Me

In this year-long unit, students will study changes in themselves. They will collect data, evaluate and interpret that data, and make graphs to display the data. In culminating activities, students will create illustrated stories and multimedia projects about themselves compared to others. The units in this theme can be completed as a whole or as individual parts.

STANDARDS MET IN THIS UNIT

NETS 3, 4, 5, 6
Math 1, 4, 5
Social Studies Ivf

WEB RESOURCES

Growth
    Are You Taller in the Morning?:
       www.shu.ac.uk/schools/sci/sol/invest/height/height.htm
    BodyQuest: http://library.thinkquest.org/10348/
    BrainPOP—Growth and Genetics:
       www.brainpop.com/health/growthanddevelopment/
    Flintstones Growth Chart: www.flintstonesvitamins.ca/kids/growth/home.html
    Growth Chart: www.chennaikids.com/growthchart/growthchart.shtml

SOFTWARE

Excel or Appleworks
HyperStudio
PowerPoint
Word or Appleworks

MONTHS 1 THROUGH 6

Students measure individual heights on a monthly basis throughout the year. Records are kept on a spreadsheet. A close-up digital photo will be taken once per month to show changes in facial structure and appearance. The students will write a description of the changes that take place.

MONTH 7

Near the year's end, children create graphs to show their progress. They find the averages of change for the class and (as subsets) for boys and girls. They find the differences between their own growth and the class's average, and the average for their gender. Each student types a one page reflection on how they have changed during the months.

MONTH 8

Students will create animated GIF images of their photos as they changed throughout the year, and include them in a multimedia presentation on individual changes and the class's changes.

ASSESSMENT   Develop an assessment rubric that covers the following criteria, adding your own criteria:

Content
- evidence of understanding of measurement
- evidence of understanding of change and growth
- reflection paper
- neatness
- accuracy

Technology
- use of digital camera
- use of spreadsheet
- use of word processor
- use of multimedia application

For help in creating rubrics, use as a resource the "Constructing a Rubric" essay found in the Strategies for Getting Started chapter of this book.

Change and My School

In this year-long unit, students will study changes in their school. They will collect data, evaluate and interpret that data, and make graphs to display the data. In culminating activities, students will create illustrated stories and multimedia projects about their school. These units can be completed as a whole or as individual parts.

STANDARDS MET
IN THIS UNIT

NETS 3, 4, 5, 6
English Language Arts 7
Math 1, 4, 5
Social Studies IIIi

WEB RESOURCES

Seasons
    BrainPOP—Seasons: www.brainpop.com/science/weather/seasons/index.weml
    Four Seasons at the Farm: www.redbudfarms.com/hist.four.seasons.htm
    New Science—A Change of Seasons:
      http://liftoff.msfc.nasa.gov/news/2001/news-autumnalequinox.asp
    New Science—The First Day of Spring:
      http://kids.msfc.nasa.gov/News/2000/News-VernalEquinox.asp
    The Wonderful World of Trees: www.domtar.com/arbre/english/start.htm

SOFTWARE

Excel or Appleworks
HyperStudio
PowerPoint
Word or Appleworks

MONTHS 1
THROUGH 6

Digital photos and measurements should be taken of the school environment. These photos and measurements can include tree and plant growth, building construction, and playground improvements. Temperature and rainfall measurements should also be taken at the school. Records are kept on a spreadsheet.

MONTH 7

Near the year's end, children create graphs to show the changes. They find the averages of change. Each student types a one page reflection on how things have changed during the months.

MONTH 8

The final product would be a book created on HyperStudio, PowerPoint, CD-ROM, disk, or word processor. Children work in small groups to focus on one aspect of change at the school and present their findings on a series of slides or cards. The work from all groups will be put together in one multimedia presentation.

ASSESSMENT

Develop an assessment rubric that covers the following criteria, adding your own criteria:

Content

- evidence of understanding of measurement
- evidence of understanding of change and growth
- reflection paper
- neatness
- accuracy

Technology

- use of digital camera
- use of spreadsheet
- use of word processor
- use of multimedia application

For help in creating rubrics, use as a resource the "Constructing a Rubric" essay found in the Strategies for Getting Started chapter of this book.

Change and My Community

In this year-long unit, students will study changes in the community around them. They will collect data, evaluate and interpret that data, and make graphs to display the data. In culminating activities, students will create illustrated stories and multimedia projects about their community. These units can be completed as a whole or as individual parts.

STANDARDS MET IN THIS UNIT

NETS 3, 4, 5
English Language Arts 4, 8
Math 1, 4, 5
Social Studies IIIi

WEB RESOURCES

Community
   Build a Community:
      www.pbs.org/klru/forgottenamericans/buildcomm/community.htm
   Hometown Heroes: www.weta.org/productions/hheroes/
   Italian-American Traditions:
      www.balchinstitute.org/museum/italian/italian2.html
   Kids and Community: www.planning.org/kidsandcommunity/
   What Kids Can Do: www.whatkidscando.org/intro.html

SOFTWARE

Excel or Appleworks
HyperStudio
Inspiration
PowerPoint
Word or Appleworks

MONTHS 1 THROUGH 6

While examining the local community, students determine the factors (rivers, mining, timber, climate, geographical location, population, etc.) that contributed to the development of the area by using a variety of methods, including Internet searches of pertinent Web sites. Teachers will want to have students organize their findings in a format that is amenable to a multimedia presentation (see Month 8). For instance, a chart in Word or a diagram in Inspiration will identify a community "factor" such as a river and note how that factor has contributed to the development and historical change of the community. Students may also want to use local news sources to document the ways people support one another in the community.

Each month for the next six months, students find the average temperature, rainfall, and air quality indexes for your community. They should record their data using spreadsheet software.

MONTH 7   Near the year's end, children create graphs to show the changes over time in the temperature, rainfall, and air quality indexes. Depending on their mathematics skills, they can find the average for each measure for the entire six-month period. Each student types a one-page reflection on how things have changed over the months.

MONTH 8   Create a multimedia report for the Chamber of Commerce. This report should describe the origins, features, occupations, and traditions of your town. It should also include the charts and graphs students created in Months 1 and 7. Take a persuasive point of view to explain why your community is a good place to live.

ASSESSMENT   Develop an assessment rubric that covers the following criteria, adding your own criteria:

Content
- evidence of understanding of community
- evidence of understanding of change
- reflection paper
- neatness
- accuracy

Technology
- use of digital camera
- use of spreadsheet
- use of word processor
- use of multimedia application

For help in creating rubrics, use as a resource the "Constructing a Rubric" essay found in the Strategies for Getting Started chapter of this book.

Change and Science

In this two-week, interdisciplinary unit, students will research the life cycle and migration path of the monarch butterfly. They will read books about the monarch butterfly and use this information to direct online research. From this research, students will create a virtual garden on the Web with links to appropriate Internet sites.

STANDARDS MET IN THIS UNIT

NETS 1, 3, 4, 5
English Language Arts 3, 4, 5, 7, 8, 11, 12
Science C1, C2, C3

WEB RESOURCES

Butterflies
    Children's Butterfly Site: www.mesc.nbs.gov/butterfly/Butterfly.html
    Journey North: www.learner.org/jnorth/
    Milkweed Café: www.milkweedcafe.com/
    Monarch Butterflies: www.pacificgrove.com/butterflies/index.html
    Monarch Watch: www.monarchwatch.org/
    Sharon's Monarch Butterfly Site: http://home.wi.rr.com/monarchraising/

SOFTWARE

HyperStudio
Inspiration
PowerPoint
Netscape Composer
TimeLiner

DAY 1

As an introduction, read *Monarch Butterfly* by Gail Gibbons about the life cycle of the monarch butterfly. Have a discussion about the important phases of the change from egg to butterfly. Using Inspiration, students create a brainstorm web of the areas to research about monarch butterflies.

DAYS 2 THROUGH 4

In teams, students investigate the life cycle of the monarch butterfly, conducting research online. Teachers who feel comfortable allowing their students to conduct Internet searches can explain search techniques using keywords such as "monarch butterfly". If time is an issue, teachers might want to preselect a site and even bookmark it for easy access by students.

After completing research, students will also learn the scientific vocabulary and write stories that will summarize the process of metamorphosis.

DAYS 5 THROUGH 7

In teams, students investigate the migration path of the monarch butterfly, conducting research online. This will include researching the migration paths of the monarchs, collecting a variety of books and Internet sites. Teachers who feel comfortable allowing their students to conduct Internet searches can explain search techniques using keywords such as "monarch butterfly" and "migration". If time is an issue, teachers might want to preselect a site and even bookmark it for easy access by students.

Tracking Migration

Journey North: www.learner.org/jnorth/

Journey North Teacher's Manual: www.learner.org/jnorth/tm/MapRegions.html

Monarch Watch: www.monarchwatch.org/tagmig/index.htm

Students will create a color map of this migration pattern and then scan the maps and save for the culminating project.

DAYS 8 AND 9   Students will create a multimedia presentation that will explain the monarch butterfly's life cycle and migration path. Additionally, students may create a virtual garden with links to appropriate Web sites.

ASSESSMENT   Develop an assessment rubric that covers the following criteria, adding your own criteria:

Content
- evidence of understanding of migration
- use of scientific vocabulary
- color map
- time line
- neatness

Technology
- access of Web resources
- use of Inspiration
- use of TimeLiner 4.0
- use of multimedia application

For help in creating rubrics, use as a resource the "Constructing a Rubric" essay found in the Strategies for Getting Started chapter of this book.

Change and Social Studies

In this unit, the students examine change in civil rights during the past century. Students will conduct Internet research to determine how both women and minorities have gained equality under the law over time. By applying their understanding of change to their local community, students will conduct interviews and document local history in a multimedia presentation.

STANDARDS MET IN THIS UNIT

NETS 2, 3, 4, 5, 6
Social Studies I e, II a, c, IV h, V d, VI a, f

WEB RESOURCES

Women
Military Women Veterans: http://userpages.aug.com/captbarb/
History of Women's Suffrage: www.rochester.edu/SBA/history.html
Not for Ourselves Alone: www.pbs.org/stantonanthony/
Time for Kids—Women's History Month:
  www.timeforkids.com/TFK/specials/0,6709,101044,00.html
Woman's Suffrage and the 19th Amendment:
  www.nara.gov/education/teaching/woman/home.html

Minorities
America's Jim Crow Laws: www.ushmm.org/olympics/zcc036a.htm
Our Shared History: www.cr.nps.gov/aahistory/
Powerful Days: www.civilrightsphotos.com/Pages/index2.html
Stand Up for Your Rights: www.pbs.org/wgbh/amex/kids/civilrights/
Time line of the American Civil Rights Movement:
  www.wmich.edu/politics/mlk/

SOFTWARE

HyperStudio
PowerPoint
TimeLiner

DAYS 1 AND 2

Students study Web sites about rights for women and minorities listed above and discuss how rights for these groups of Americans have changed during the past century. Have students work in small groups using TimeLiner to create a virtual time line of women or minority achievements throughout the past 100 years. Share time lines with the class.

DAYS 3 AND 4

Students research local history throughout the past 100 years through Web-based archives and/or a field trip to the local library to use records housed there. Notes will be kept on significant local figures and events that are recorded in local news sources.

DAY 5   As a class, students discuss their research findings and identify significant local news stories pertaining to civil rights during the past century. Students in small groups volunteer to further study specific names or events.

DAYS 6
THROUGH 8   Students work in small groups to continue research, including at least one interview with local citizens who can share memories of how their roles as women or minorities have changed in their life times. The person should be at least 50 years old and ideally will agree to have a digital picture taken.

DAYS 9 AND 10   Students work in small groups to prepare multimedia presentations on their findings and share with the group.

ASSESSMENT   Develop an assessment rubric that covers the following criteria, adding your own criteria:

Content
- evidence of understanding of civil rights
- evidence of understanding of how to use a time line
- interview of local citizen
- neatness
- accuracy

Technology
- access Web resources
- Web-based or library research
- use of digital camera
- use of multimedia application

For help in creating rubrics, use as a resource the "Constructing a Rubric" essay found in the Strategies for Getting Started chapter of this book

culminating
event

Community Virtual Tour

Students work in small groups to create a community virtual tour on a Web site. Each section of the site will allow visitors to experience the school, community, history and people of the local region. Each component of the Web site should be interactive and emphasize the theme of change, including links to additional Web resources on its topic.

OR

Each student selects one of his/her work products and showcases it at a daylong community history forum. Students can select roles as historians, reporters, advocates or historical figures, presenting their work to one another in the morning, and then students from other classes can be scheduled in throughout the day to view the exhibit. Parents and the general community can attend, too.

Each student should stay in character and provide an interactive experience for interested visitors. Have a podium with a microphone and schedule a debate on how your community has changed as the highpoint of the day.

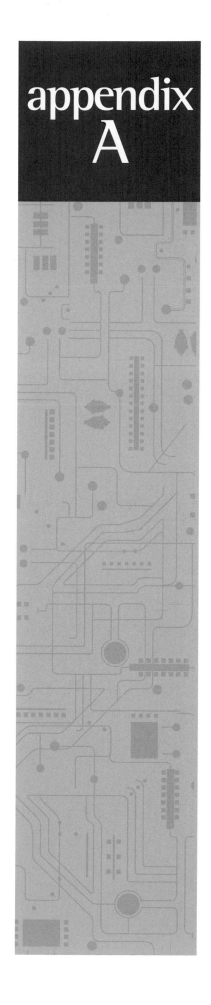

appendix A

Assessment Rubrics

Blank Assessment Rubric Template

CRITERIA	1 UNSATISFACTORY	2 SATISFACTORY	3 EXEMPLARY	TOTAL

Social Studies Project Rubric

CRITERIA	1 UNSATISFACTORY	2 SATISFACTORY	3 EXEMPLARY	TOTAL
Created presentation in a clean, easy to follow format.	Messy, hard to read or understand.	Presentation was clean, neat and easy to follow.	Presentation was clean, easy to follow and provided a greater understanding of the grievances.	
Included 7 or more events that occurred between 1763 and 1775.	Presentation contained fewer than 7 events or contained fictional events.	Presentation included 7 historic events that occurred between 1763 and 1775.	Presentation included more than 7 historic events between 1763 and 1775.	
Explained how each event was a justified grievance from the colonists' point of view.	Listed events without explaining their impact on colonists.	Explained how each event was a justified grievance from the colonists' point of view.	Explained how each event was a justified grievance and showed how each event built on previous resentments.	
Presented the final product to the class successfully.	Presented an incomplete or inaccurate presentation.	Presented a presentation that successfully explained the colonists' grievances.	Presented a presentation that successfully explained the colonists' grievances and successfully answered audience questions on the subject.	

Lesson Plan Evaluation Rubric

CRITERIA	EXCELLENT	ADEQUATE	UNSATISFACTORY
Images	8-10 images are digitized. Images are clear, visually appealing and consistent in size, downloaded into the software program, and filed appropriately.	6-8 images are digitized and/or the images are clear. Some lack appeal and are not consistent in size. Some may not be filed appropriately.	Images are provided, but not digitized, are unclear, and/or may not be consistent in size. The candidate has not filed the images for future use.
Sorting of Images (Venn Diagram)	The Venn diagram is done using a computer program. All circles are appropriately labeled. All items are in the appropriate spots.	The Venn diagram might not be done with a computer program, some elements are inappropriately labeled or the items are not appropriately placed.	The Venn diagram is hand drawn, elements are not in appropriate places, parts not labeled.
Questions	A hierarchical list of questions is provided with each type of question labeled. Scaffolding comments are provided between the levels.	A list of questions is provided, but the hierarchy is not appropriate and/or the scaffolding comments are inappropriate or absent.	A list of questions is provided, not related to young children, not sequenced, and no scaffolding evident.
Lesson Plan	The lesson plan notes a specific student population, identifies appropriate resources, defines an effective plan for managing the instruction and resources in exploring the curriculum and assessing student learning.	The lesson plan is mechanical in nature, providing an outcome, but no thought as to what the teacher does, the student is required to do, and what the pitfalls and possibilities are.	The lesson plan does not specify student population, resources, or management.
Reflection/ Journal	The focus is on personal feelings, skills needed for planning and teaching, and how they can use this experience with young students.	The focus is on personal feelings and some on the skills that are needed for planning and teaching.	The focus of the reflection is on how they liked the lesson.

PowerPoint Rubric

This rubric may be used for self-assessment and peer feedback. The project grade will be based upon the following evaluation scale:

A – Exemplary: 32-29 points
B – Proficient: 28-22 points
Partially Proficient or Incomplete (needs to be resubmitted): Less than 22 points

ACTIVITY	EXEMPLARY	PROFICIENT	PARTIALLY PROFICIENT	INCOMPLETE	POINTS
Research and Notetaking	6 points Notecards indicate group members accurately researched varied information sources, recorded and interpreted statements, graphics and questions and evaluated alternative points of view.	4 points Notecards show group members recorded relevant information from multiple sources of information, evaluated and synthesized relevant information.	2 points Notecards show group members recorded relevant information from multiple sources of information, evaluated and synthesized relevant information.	0 points Notecards show group members recorded information from four or fewer resources, and ignored alternative points of view.	
Preproduction Plan— Storyboard	6 points The storyboard illustrates the slide presentation structure with thumbnail sketches of each slide including: title of slide, text, background color, placement and size of graphic, fonts (color, size), type for text and headings, hyperlinks (list URLs of any site linked from the slide), narration text, and audio files (if any). All slides are numbered, and there is a logical sequence to the presentation.	4 points The thumbnail sketches on the storyboard include titles and text for each slide and are in sequential order.	2 points The thumbnail sketches on the storyboard are not in a logical sequence and have incomplete information.	0 points There are a very few thumbnail sketches on the storyboard and do not provide an overview of the presentation.	

PowerPoint Rubric, continued

ACTIVITY	EXEMPLARY	PROFICIENT	PARTIALLY PROFICIENT	INCOMPLETE	POINTS
Content	**8 points** The content is written clearly and concisely with a logical progression of ideas and supporting information. The project includes motivating questions and advanced organizers that provide the audience with sense of the project's main idea. Information is accurate, current and comes mainly from primary sources.*	**6 points** The content is written with a logical progression of ideas and supporting information. Includes persuasive information from primary sources.*	**4 points** The content is vague in conveying a point of view and does not create a strong sense of purpose. Includes some persuasive information with few facts. Some of the information may not seem to fit. Use of primary sources* is not always clear.	**0 points** The content lacks a clear point of view and logical sequence of information. Includes little persuasive information and only one or two facts about the topic. Information is incomplete, out of date and/or incorrect. Sequencing of ideas is unclear.	
Layout	**3 points** The layout is aesthetically pleasing and contributes to the overall message with appropriate use of headings and subheadings and white space.	**2 points** The layout uses horizontal and vertical white space appropriately.	**1 point** The layout shows some structure, but appears cluttered and busy or distracting with large gaps of white space or uses a distracting background.	**0 points** The layout is cluttered, confusing, and does not use spacing, headings and subheadings to enhance the readability.	
Citations	**6 points** Sources of information are properly cited so that the audience can determine the credibility and authority of the information presented. All sources of information are clearly identified and credited using MLA citations throughout the project.	**4 points** Most sources of information use proper MLA citation, and sources are documented to make it possible to check on the accuracy of information.	**2 points** Sometimes copyright guidelines are followed and some information, photos and graphics do not use proper MLA citations.	**0 points** No way to check validity of information.	

* Primary sources can include original letters and diaries, personal observations, interviews, first-hand accounts, newspaper articles, magazine articles, journal articles, Web pages, audio recordings, video productions, and photography.

PowerPoint Rubric, continued

ACTIVITY	EXEMPLARY	PROFICIENT	PARTIALLY PROFICIENT	INCOMPLETE	POINTS
Graphics, Sound, and Animation	3 points The graphics, sound and/or animation assist in presenting an overall theme and make visual connections that enhance understanding of concept, ideas and relationships. Original images are created using proper size and resolution, and all images enhance the content. There is a consistent visual theme.	2 points The graphics, sound/and or animation visually depict material and assist the audience in understanding the flow of information or content. Original images are used. Images are proper size, resolution.	1 point Some of the graphics, sounds, and/or animations seem unrelated to the topic/theme and do not enhance the overall concepts. Most images are clipart or recycled from the WWW. Images are too large/small in size. Images are poorly cropped or the color/resolution is fuzzy.	0 points The graphics, sounds, and/or animations are unrelated to the content. Graphics do not enhance understanding of the content, or are distracting decorations that create a busy feeling and detract from the content.	
				TOTAL POINTS	

Measurement and Statistics Rubric

CRITERIA	0	1	2	3
Graph title	No title.	Title does not relate to graph.	Title relates to graph. Capitalization or spelling error present	Title relates to graph. Capitalization and spelling are perfect
Axes labeled	No labels.	Labels do not relate to graph.	Labels relate to graph. Capitalization or spelling error present.	Labels relate to graph. Capitalization and spelling are perfect.
X-axis information	Not present.	Information present but inappropriate.	Information present with errors.	Information present and accurate.
Y-axis information	Not present.	Axis numbered incorrectly.	Axis numbered correctly.	Axis numbered correctly and neatly.
Graph accuracy	Incomplete.	Graph complete but inaccurate.	Graph complete and accurate.	Graph complete, accurate, and neat.

Evaluator: _____

Points possible = 15

Points earned = _____

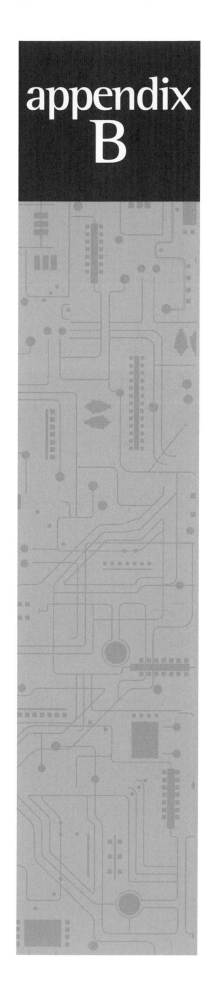

appendix B

Standards

NATIONAL EDUCATIONAL TECHNOLOGY STANDARDS
FOR STUDENTS (NETS•S)

NATIONAL EDUCATIONAL TECHNOLOGY STANDARDS
FOR TEACHERS (NETS•T)

ENGLISH LANGUAGE ARTS STANDARDS

SOCIAL STUDIES STANDARDS

MATHEMATICS STANDARDS

SCIENCE STANDARDS

National Educational Technology Standards for Students

1. BASIC OPERATIONS AND CONCEPTS
- Students demonstrate a sound understanding of the nature and operation of technology systems.
- Students are proficient in the use of technology.

2. SOCIAL, ETHICAL, AND HUMAN ISSUES
- Students understand the ethical, cultural, and societal issues related to technology.
- Students practice responsible use of technology systems, information, and software.
- Students develop positive attitudes toward technology uses that support lifelong learning, collaboration, personal pursuits, and productivity.

3. TECHNOLOGY PRODUCTIVITY TOOLS
- Students use technology tools to enhance learning, increase productivity, and promote creativity.
- Students use productivity tools to collaborate in constructing technology-enhanced models, preparing publications, and producing other creative works.

4. TECHNOLOGY COMMUNICATIONS TOOLS
- Students use telecommunications to collaborate, publish, and interact with peers, experts, and other audiences.
- Students use a variety of media and formats to communicate information and ideas effectively to multiple audiences.

5. TECHNOLOGY RESEARCH TOOLS
- Students use technology to locate, evaluate, and collect information from a variety of sources.
- Students use technology tools to process data and report results.
- Students evaluate and select new information resources and technological innovations based on the appropriateness to specific tasks.

6. TECHNOLOGY PROBLEM-SOLVING AND DECISION-MAKING TOOLS
- Students use technology resources for solving problems and making informed decisions.
- Students employ technology in the development of strategies for solving problems in the real world.

National Educational Technology Standards (NETS) for Teachers

All classroom teachers should be prepared to meet the following standards and performance indicators.

I. TECHNOLOGY OPERATIONS AND CONCEPTS

Teachers demonstrate a sound understanding of technology operations and concepts. Teachers:

    A. demonstrate introductory knowledge, skills, and understanding of concepts related to technology (as described in the ISTE National Educational Technology Standards for Students).

    B. demonstrate continual growth in technology knowledge and skills to stay abreast of current and emerging technologies.

II. PLANNING AND DESIGNING LEARNING ENVIRONMENTS AND EXPERIENCES

Teachers plan and design effective learning environments and experiences supported by technology. Teachers:

    A. design developmentally appropriate learning opportunities that apply technology-enhanced instructional strategies to support the diverse needs of learners.

    B. apply current research on teaching and learning with technology when planning learning environments and experiences.

    C. identify and locate technology resources and evaluate them for accuracy and suitability.

    D. plan for the management of technology resources within the context of learning activities.

    E. plan strategies to manage student learning in a technology-enhanced environment.

III. TEACHING, LEARNING, AND THE CURRICULUM

Teachers implement curriculum plans that include methods and strategies for applying technology to maximize student learning. Teachers

    A. facilitate technology-enhanced experiences that address content standards and student technology standards.

    B. use technology to support learner-centered strategies that address the diverse needs of students.

    C. apply technology to develop students' higher-order skills and creativity.

    D. manage student learning activities in a technology-enhanced environment.

IV. ASSESSMENT AND EVALUATION

Teachers apply technology to facilitate a variety of effective assessment and evaluation strategies. Teachers:

    A. apply technology in assessing student learning of subject matter using a variety of assessment techniques.

    B. use technology resources to collect and analyze data, interpret results, and communicate findings to improve instructional practice and maximize student learning.

    C. apply multiple methods of evaluation to determine students' appropriate use of technology resources for learning, communication, and productivity.

V. PRODUCTIVITY AND PROFESSIONAL PRACTICE

Teachers use technology to enhance their productivity and professional practice. Teachers:

A. use technology resources to engage in ongoing professional development and lifelong learning.

B. continually evaluate and reflect on professional practice to make informed decisions regarding the use of technology in support of student learning.

C. apply technology to increase productivity.

D. use technology to communicate and collaborate with peers, parents, and the larger community in order to nurture student learning.

VI. SOCIAL, ETHICAL, LEGAL, AND HUMAN ISSUES

Teachers understand the social, ethical, legal, and human issues surrounding the use of technology in PK–12 schools and apply that understanding in practice. Teachers:

A. model and teach legal and ethical practice related to technology use.

B. apply technology resources to enable and empower learners with diverse backgrounds, characteristics, and abilities.

C. identify and use technology resources that affirm diversity.

D. promote safe and healthy use of technology resources.

E. facilitate equitable access to technology resources for all students.

English Language Arts Standards

The vision guiding these standards is that all students must have the opportunities and resources to develop the language skills they need to pursue life's goals and to participate fully as informed, productive members of society. These standards assume that literacy growth begins before children enter school as they experience and experiment with literacy activities—reading and writing, and associating spoken words with their graphic representations. Recognizing this fact, these standards encourage the development of curriculum and instruction that make productive use of the emerging literacy abilities that children bring to school. Furthermore, the standards provide ample room for the innovation and creativity essential to teaching and learning. They are not prescriptions for particular curricula or instruction.

Although we present these standards as a list, we want to emphasize that they are not distinct and separable; they are, in fact, interrelated and should be considered as a whole.

1. *Students read a wide range of print and nonprint texts to build an understanding of texts, of themselves, and of the cultures of the United States and the world; to acquire new information; to respond to the needs and demands of society and the workplace; and for personal fulfillment. Among these texts are fiction and nonfiction, classic and contemporary works.*

2. *Students read a wide range of literature from many periods in many genres to build an understanding of the many dimensions (e.g., philosophical, ethical, and aesthetic) of human experience.*

3. *Students apply a wide range of strategies to comprehend, interpret, evaluate, and appreciate texts. They draw on their prior experience, their interactions with other readers and writers, their knowledge of word meaning and of other texts, their word identification strategies, and their understanding of textual features (e.g., sound-letter correspondence, sentence structure, context, and graphics).*

4. *Students adjust their use of spoken, written, and visual language (e.g., conventions, style, and vocabulary) to communicate effectively with a variety of audiences and for different purposes.*

5. *Students employ a wide range of strategies as they write and use different writing process elements appropriately to communicate with different audiences for a variety of purposes.*

6. *Students apply knowledge of language structure, language conventions (e.g., spelling and punctuation), media techniques, figurative language, and genre to create, critique, and discuss print and nonprint texts.*

7. *Students conduct research on issues and interests by generating ideas and questions, and by posing problems. They gather, evaluate, and synthesize data from a variety of sources (e.g., print and nonprint texts, artifacts, and people) to communicate their discoveries in ways that suit their purpose and audience.*

8. *Students use a variety of technological and information resources (e.g., libraries, databases, computer networks, and video) to gather and synthesize information and to*

create and communicate knowledge.

9. Students develop an understanding of and respect for diversity in language use, patterns, and dialects across cultures, ethnic groups, geographic regions, and social roles.

10. Students whose first language is not English make use of their first language to develop competency in the English language arts and to develop understanding of content across the curriculum.

11. Students participate as knowledgeable, reflective, creative, and critical members of a variety of literacy communities.

12. Students use spoken, written, and visual language to accomplish their own purposes (e.g., for learning, enjoyment, persuasion, and the exchange of information).

math

Mathematics Standards

STANDARD 1: NUMBER AND OPERATIONS
Instructional programs from PK–12 should enable all students to—
- understand numbers, ways of representing numbers, relationships among numbers, and number systems;
- understand meanings of operations and how they relate to one another;
- compute fluently and make reasonable estimates.

STANDARD 2: ALGEBRA
Instructional programs from PK–12 should enable all students to—
- understand patterns, relations, and functions;
- represent and analyze mathematical situations and structures using algebraic symbols;
- use mathematical models to represent and understand quantitative relationships;
- analyze change in various contexts.

STANDARD 3: GEOMETRY
Instructional programs from PK–12 should enable all students to—
- analyze characteristics and properties of two- and three-dimensional geometric shapes and develop mathematical arguments about geometric relationships;
- specify locations and describe spatial relationships using coordinate geometry and other representational systems;
- apply transformations and use symmetry to analyze mathematical situations;
- use visualization, spatial reasoning, and geometric modeling to solve problems.

STANDARD 4: MEASUREMENT
Instructional programs from PK–12 should enable all students to—
- understand measurable attributes of objects and the units, systems, and processes of measurement;
- apply appropriate techniques, tools, and formulas to determine measurements.

STANDARD 5: DATA ANALYSIS AND PROBABILITY
Instructional programs from PK–12 should enable all students to—
- formulate questions that can be addressed with data and collect, organize, and display relevant data to answer them;
- select and use appropriate statistical methods to analyze data;
- develop and evaluate inferences and predictions that are based on data;
- understand and apply basic concepts of probability.

STANDARD 6: PROBLEM SOLVING
Instructional programs from PK–12 should enable all students to—
- build new mathematical knowledge through problem solving;
- solve problems that arise in mathematics and in other contexts;

- apply and adapt a variety of appropriate strategies to solve problems;
- monitor and reflect on the process of mathematical problem solving.

Reprinted with permission from Principles and Standards for School Mathematics. *Copyright 2000 by the National Council of Teachers of Mathematics. Available online: http://standards.nctm.org.*

STANDARD 7: REASONING AND PROOF
Instructional programs from PK–12 should enable all students to—
- recognize reasoning and proof as fundamental aspects of mathematics;
- make and investigate mathematical conjectures;
- develop and evaluate mathematical arguments and proofs;
- select and use various types of reasoning and methods of proof.

STANDARD 8: COMMUNICATION
Instructional programs from PK–12 should enable all students to—
- organize and consolidate their mathematical thinking through communication;
- communicate their mathematical thinking coherently and clearly to peers, teachers, and others;
- analyze and evaluate the mathematical thinking and strategies of others;
- use the language of mathematics to express mathematical ideas precisely.

STANDARD 9: CONNECTIONS
Instructional programs from PK–12 should enable all students to—
- recognize and use connections among mathematical ideas;
- understand how mathematical ideas interconnect and build on one another to produce a coherent whole;
- recognize and apply mathematics in contexts outside of mathematics.

STANDARD 10: REPRESENTATION
Instructional programs from PK–12 should enable all students to—
- create and use representations to organize, record, and communicate mathematical ideas;
- select, apply, and translate among mathematical representations to solve problems;
- use representations to model and interpret physical, social, and mathematical phenomena.

Science Standards

Grades K–12

CONTENT STANDARD: UNIFYING CONCEPTS AND PROCESSES
As a result of activities in Grades K–12, all students should develop understanding and abilities aligned with the following concepts and processes:

- Systems, order, and organization
- Evidence, models, and explanation
- Constancy, change, and measurement
- Evolution and equilibrium
- Form and function

Grades K–4

CONTENT STANDARD A: SCIENCE AS INQUIRY
A1. Abilities necessary to do scientific inquiry:

- Ask a question about objects, organisms, and events in the environment.
- Plan and conduct a simple investigation.
- Employ simple equipment and tools to gather data and extend the senses.
- Use data to construct a reasonable explanation.
- Communicate investigations and explanations.

A2. Understanding about scientific inquiry:

- Scientific investigations involve asking and answering a question and comparing the answer with what scientists already know about the world.
- Scientists use different kinds of investigations depending on the questions they are trying to answer.
- Simple instruments provide more information than scientists obtain using only their senses.
- Scientists develop explanations using observations (evidence) and what they already know about the world (scientific knowledge).
- Scientists make the results of their investigations public; they describe the investigations in ways that enable others to repeat the investigations.
- Scientists review and ask questions about the results of other scientists' work.

CONTENT STANDARD B: PHYSICAL SCIENCE
B1. Properties of objects and materials
B2. Position and motion of objects
B3. Light, heat, electricity, and magnetism

CONTENT STANDARD C: LIFE SCIENCE
C1. The characteristics of organisms
C2. Life cycles of organisms
C3. Organisms and environments

Reprinted with permission from National Science Education Standards. *Copyright 1996 by the National Academy of Sciences. Courtesy of the National Academy Press, Washington, D.C.*

CONTENT STANDARD D: EARTH AND SPACE SCIENCE

D1. Properties of earth materials

D2. Objects in the sky

D3. Changes in earth and sky

CONTENT STANDARD E: SCIENCE AND TECHNOLOGY

E1. Abilities of technological design

E2. Understanding about science and technology

E3. Abilities to distinguish between natural objects and objects made by humans

CONTENT STANDARD F: SCIENCE IN PERSONAL AND SOCIAL PERSPECTIVES

F1. Personal health

F2. Characteristics and changes in populations

F3. Types of resources

F4. Changes in environments

F5. Science and technology in local challenges

CONTENT STANDARD G: HISTORY AND NATURE OF SCIENCE

G1. Science as a human endeavor:

- Science and technology have been practiced by people for a long time.
- Men and women have made a variety of contributions throughout the history of science and technology.
- Science will never be finished.
- Many people choose science as a career.

Grades 5–8 Standards

CONTENT STANDARD A: SCIENCE AS INQUIRY

A1. Abilities necessary to do scientific inquiry:

- Identify questions that can be answered through scientific investigations.
- Design and conduct a scientific investigation.
- Use appropriate tools and techniques to gather, analyze, and interpret data.
- Develop descriptions, explanations, predictions, and models using evidence and explanations.
- Recognize and analyze alternative explanations and predictions.
- Communicate scientific procedures and explanations.
- Use mathematics in all aspects of scientific inquiry.

A2. Understanding about scientific inquiry:

- Different kinds of questions suggest different kinds of scientific investigations.
- Current scientific knowledge and understanding guide scientific investigations.
- Mathematics is important in all aspects of scientific inquiry.
- Technology used to gather data enhances accuracy and allows scientists to analyze and quantify results of investigations.
- Scientific explanations emphasize evidence, have logically consistent arguments, and use scientific principles, models, and theories.
- Science advances through legitimate skepticism.
- Scientific investigations sometimes result in new ideas and phenomena.

CONTENT STANDARD B: PHYSICAL SCIENCE
B1. Properties and changes of properties in matter

B2. Motion and forces

B3. Transfer of energy

CONTENT STANDARD C: LIFE SCIENCE
C1. Structure and function in living systems

C2. Reproduction and heredity

C3. Regulation and behavior

C4. Populations and ecosystems

C5. Diversity and adaptations of organisms

CONTENT STANDARD D: EARTH AND SPACE SCIENCE
D1. Structure of the earth system

D2. Earth's history

D3. Earth in the solar system

CONTENT STANDARD E: SCIENCE AND TECHNOLOGY
E1. Abilities of technological design:

- Identify appropriate problems for technological design.
- Design a solution or product.
- Implement a proposed design.
- Evaluate completed technological designs or products.
- Communicate the process of technological design.

E2. Understanding about science and technology:

- Scientific inquiry and technological design have similarities and differences.
- Many different people in different cultures have made and continue to make contributions to science and technology.
- Science and technology are reciprocal.
- Perfectly designed solutions do not exist.
- Technological designs have constraints.
- Technological solutions have intended benefits and unintended consequences.

CONTENT STANDARD F: SCIENCE IN PERSONAL AND SOCIAL PERSPECTIVES
F1. Personal health

F2. Populations, resources, and environments

F3. Natural hazards

F4. Risks and benefits

F5. Science and technology in society

CONTENT STANDARD G: HISTORY AND NATURE OF SCIENCE
G1. Science as a human endeavor:

- Women and men of various social and ethnic backgrounds engage in the activities of science, engineering, and related fields.
- Science requires different abilities.

G2. Nature of science:

- Scientists formulate and test their explanations of nature using observation, experiments, and theoretical and mathematical models.

- It is normal for scientists to differ with one another about the interpretation of the evidence or theory being considered.
- It is part of scientific inquiry to evaluate ideas proposed by other scientists.

G3. History of science:

- Many individuals have contributed to the traditions of science.
- In historical perspective, science has been practiced by different individuals in different cultures.
- Tracing the history of science can show how difficult it was for scientific innovators to break through the accepted ideas of their time to reach the conclusions that we currently take for granted.

social studies

Social Studies Standards

Performance Expectations for the Early Grades

I. CULTURE

Social studies programs should include experiences that provide for the study of culture and cultural diversity, so that the learner can:

a. explore and describe similarities and differences in the ways groups, societies, and cultures address similar human needs and concerns;

b. give examples of how experiences may be interpreted differently by people from diverse cultural perspectives and frames of reference;

c. describe ways in which language, stories, folktales, music, and artistic creations serve as expressions of culture and influence behavior of people living in a particular culture;

d. compare ways in which people from different cultures think about and deal with their physical environment and social conditions;

e. give examples and describe the importance of cultural unity and diversity within and across groups.

II. TIME, CONTINUITY, AND CHANGE

Social studies programs should include experiences that provide for the study of the ways human beings view themselves in and over time, so that the learner can:

a. demonstrate an understanding that different people may describe the same event or situation in diverse ways, citing reasons for the differences in views;

b. demonstrate an ability to use correctly vocabulary associated with time such as past, present, future, and long ago; read and construct simple timelines; identify examples of change; and recognize examples of cause and effect relationships;

c. compare and contrast different stories or accounts about past events, people, places, or situations, identifying how they contribute to our understanding of the past;

d. identify and use various sources for reconstructing the past, such as documents, letters, diaries, maps, textbooks, photos, and others;

e. demonstrate an understanding that people in different times and places view the world differently;

f. use knowledge of facts and concepts drawn from history, along with elements of historical inquiry, to inform decision making about and action-taking on public issues.

III. PEOPLE, PLACES, AND ENVIRONMENTS

Social studies programs should include experiences that provide for the study of people, places, and environments, so that the learner can:

a. construct and use mental maps of locales, regions, and the world that demonstrate understanding of relative location, direction, size, and shape;

b. interpret, use, and distinguish various representations of the earth, such as maps, globes, and photographs;

c. use appropriate resources, data sources, and geographic tools such as atlases, databases, grid systems, charts, graphs, and maps to generate, manipulate, and interpret information;

d. estimate distances and calculate scale;

e. locate and distinguish among varying landforms and geographic features, such as mountains, plateaus, islands, and oceans;

f. describe and speculate about physical system changes, such as seasons, climate and weather, and the water cycle;

g. describe how people create places that reflect ideas, personality, culture, and wants and needs as they design homes, playgrounds, classrooms, and the like;

h. examine the interaction of human beings and their physical environment, the use of land, building of cities, and ecosystem changes in selected locales and regions;

i. explore ways that the earth's physical features have changed over time in the local region and beyond and how these changes may be connected to one another;

j. observe and speculate about social and economic effects of environmental changes and crises resulting from phenomena such as floods, storms, and drought;

k. consider existing uses and propose and evaluate alternative uses of resources and land in home, school, community, the region, and beyond.

IV. INDIVIDUAL DEVELOPMENT AND IDENTITY
Social studies programs should include experiences that provide for the study of individual development and identity, so that the learner can:

a. describe personal changes over time, such as those related to physical development and personal interests;

b. describe personal connections to place—especially place as associated with immediate surroundings;

c. describe the unique features of one's nuclear and extended families;

d. show how learning and physical development affect behavior;

e. identify and describe ways family, groups, and community influence the individual's daily life and personal choices;

f. explore factors that contribute to one's personal identity such as interests, capabilities, and perceptions;

g. analyze a particular event to identify reasons individuals might respond to it in different ways;

h. work independently and cooperatively to accomplish goals.

V. INDIVIDUALS, GROUPS, AND INSTITUTIONS
Social studies programs should include experiences that provide for the study of interactions among individuals, groups, and institutions, so that the learner can:

a. identify roles as learned behavior patterns in group situations such as student, family member, peer play group member, or club member;

b. give examples of and explain group and institutional influences such as religious beliefs, laws, and peer pressure, on people, events, and elements of culture;

c. identify examples of institutions and describe the interactions of people with institutions;

d. identify and describe examples of tensions between and among individuals, groups, or institutions, and how belonging to more than one group can cause internal conflicts;

e. identify and describe examples of tension between an individual's beliefs and government policies and laws;

f. give examples of the role of institutions in furthering both continuity and change;

g. show how groups and institutions work to meet individual needs and promote the common good, and identify examples of where they fail to do so.

VI. POWER, AUTHORITY, AND GOVERNANCE
Social studies programs should include experiences that provide for the study of how people create and change structures of power, authority, and governance, so that the learner can:

a. examine the rights and responsibilities of the individual in relation to his or her social group, such as family, peer group, and school class;

b. explain the purpose of government;

c. give examples of how government does or does not provide for needs and wants of people, establish order and security, and manage conflict;

d. recognize how groups and organizations encourage unity and deal with diversity to maintain order and security;

e. distinguish among local, state, and national government and identify representative leaders at these levels such as mayor, governor, and president;

f. identify and describe factors that contribute to cooperation and cause disputes within and among groups and nations;

g. explore the role of technology in communications, transportation, information-processing, weapons development, or other areas as it contributes to or helps resolve conflicts;

h. recognize and give examples of the tensions between the wants and needs of individuals and groups, and concepts such as fairness, equity, and justice.

VII. PRODUCTION, DISTRIBUTION, AND CONSUMPTION

Social studies programs should include experiences that provide for the study of how people organize for the production, distribution, and consumption of goods and services, so that the learner can:

a. give examples that show how scarcity and choice govern our economic decisions;

b. distinguish between needs and wants;

c. identify examples of private and public goods and services;

d. give examples of the various institutions that make up economic systems such as families, workers, banks, labor unions, government agencies, small businesses, and large corporations;

e. describe how we depend upon workers with specialized jobs and the ways in which they contribute to the production and exchange of goods and services;

f. describe the influence of incentives, values, traditions, and habits on economic decisions;

g. explain and demonstrate the role of money in everyday life;

h. describe the relationship of price to supply and demand;

i. use economic concepts such as supply, demand, and price to help explain events in the community and nation;

j. apply knowledge of economic concepts in developing a response to a current local economic issue, such as how to reduce the flow of trash into a rapidly filling landfill.

VIII. SCIENCE, TECHNOLOGY, AND SOCIETY

Social studies programs should include experiences that provide for the study of relationships among science, technology, and society, so that the learner can:

a. identify and describe examples in which science and technology have changed the lives of people, such as in homemaking, childcare, work, transportation, and communication;

b. identify and describe examples in which science and technology have led to changes in the physical environment, such as the building of dams and levees, offshore oil drilling, medicine from rain forests, and loss of rain forests due to extraction of resources or alternative uses;

c. describe instances in which changes in values, beliefs, and attitudes have resulted from new scientific and technological knowledge, such as conservation of resources and awareness of chemicals harmful to life and the environment;

d. identify examples of laws and policies that govern scientific and technological applications, such as the Endangered Species Act and environmental protection policies;

e. suggest ways to monitor science and technology in order to protect the physical environment, individual rights, and the common good.

IX. GLOBAL CONNECTIONS

Social studies programs should include experiences that provide for the study of global connections and interdependence, so that the learner can:

a. explore ways that language, art, music, belief systems, and other cultural elements may facilitate global understanding or lead to misunderstanding;

b. give examples of conflict, cooperation, and interdependence among individuals, groups, and nations;

c. examine the effects of changing technologies on the global community;

d. explore causes, consequences, and possible solutions to persistent, contemporary, and emerging global issues, such as pollution and endangered species;

e. examine the relationships and tensions between personal wants and needs and various global concerns, such as use of imported oil, land use, and environmental protection;

f. investigate concerns, issues, standards, and conflicts related to universal human rights, such as the treatment of children, religious groups, and effects of war.

X. CIVIC IDEALS AND PRACTICES

Social studies programs should include experiences that provide for the study of the ideals, principles, and practices of citizenship in a democratic republic, so that the learner can:

a. identify key ideals of the United States' democratic republican form of government, such as individual human dignity, liberty, justice, equality, and the rule of law, and discuss their application in specific situations;

b. identify examples of rights and responsibilities of citizens;

c. locate, access, organize, and apply information about an issue of public concern from multiple points of view;

d. identify and practice selected forms of civic discussion and participation consistent with the ideals of citizens in a democratic republic;

e. explain actions citizens can take to influence public policy decisions;

f. recognize that a variety of formal and informal actors influence and shape public policy;

g. examine the influence of public opinion on personal decision making and government policy on public issues;

h. explain how public policies and citizen behaviors may or may not reflect the stated ideals of a democratic republican form of government;

i. describe how public policies are used to address issues of public concern;

j. recognize and interpret how the "common good" can be strengthened through various forms of citizen action.

Complete your library of technology standards books!

NETS for Students

National Educational Technology Standards for Students

It's the original—and still the best way to introduce these essential standards to large groups. Full-color booklet includes the entire text of the National Educational Technology Standards for Students (NETS•S), comprising the Technology Foundation Standards for Students and performance indicators.

Member Price
$5.00
Nonmembers $5.00

Book code: NETSBO-757   19 pages ISTE, 1998

NETS for Students Poster
Member Price **$2.95** Nonmembers $2.95
Code: NETSPO-757 33" x 20¹/₂" ISTE, 1999

National Educational Technology Standards for Students— Connecting Curriculum and Technology

Exactly how *does* a teacher develop and implement technology-rich activities and projects that meet curriculum and technology standards? This book, representing four years and the collective work of more than 2,000 educators, offers a solid solution to that problem. Each of its three dozen user-friendly learning activities and eight multidisciplinary units integrates technology and curriculum in a way that creates an exciting and effective whole.

Member Price
$26.95
Nonmembers $29.95

Book code: NETSB2-757
373 pages ISBN 1-56484-150-2 ISTE, 2000

NETS for Teachers

National Educational Technology Standards for Teachers

This full-color booklet introduces ISTE's Technology Standards for Teachers (NETS•T). Each standard is supported by performance indicators and profiles for General Preparation, Professional Preparation, Student Teaching/ Internship, and First-Year Teaching. *Includes bonus pull-out poster,* also sold separately.

Member Price
$13.50
Nonmembers $15.00

Book code: NETTBO-757
32 pages ISBN 1-56484-162-6 ISTE, 2000

NETS for Teachers Poster
Member Price **$5.00** Nonmembers $5.00
Code: NETTPO-757
Poster: 33" x 10¹/₄" ISBN 1-56484-163-4 ISTE, 2000

National Educational Technology Standards for Teachers— Preparing Teachers to Use Technology

Shows how teacher educators can integrate the effective use of technology into training novice and inservice teachers. Includes 32 activities on math, science, social studies, and language arts in early childhood, elementary, middle school, and secondary programs; six activities for educational foundations courses; chapters cover model strategies, technology in student teaching/internships, first-year teaching, and professional development, as well as assessing technology preparation of teachers.

Member Price
$44.95
Nonmembers $49.95

Book code: NETTB2-757
374 pages   ISBN 1-56484-173-1   ISTE, 2002

NETS for Administrators

National Educational Technology Standards for Administrators

The National Educational Technology Standards for Administrators (NETS•A) is now available in this full-color booklet. Incorporating the new Technology Standards for School Administrators (TSSA), this booklet details the role of educational leaders in improving teaching and learning through the effective use of technology. *Includes bonus pull-out poster,* also sold separately.

Member Price
$13.50
Nonmembers $15.00

Book code: NETABO-757
28 pages   ISBN 1-56484-188-X   ISTE, 2002

NETS for Administrators Poster
Member Price **$5.00** Nonmembers $5.00
Product code: NETAPO-757
Poster: 33" x 10¹/₄" ISBN 1-56484-189-8 ISTE, 2002

Susan Brooks-Young
Member Price
$40.45
Nonmember Price $44.95

Making Technology Standards Work for You—A Guide for School Administrators

A step-by-step approach to help administrators develop and implement a vision for using educational technology more effectively. Each chapter focuses on an element of educational leadership—planning, curriculum and instruction, assessment, staff development, and legal and social issues—showing how to assess what is in place already and determine what needs to be done next. The first and only book of its kind available to educational leaders.

Book code: MATECH-757
Pages 205   ISBN 1-56484-190-1   ISTE, 2002

Prices subject to change without notice.

Order these and other books by
Mail: **International Society for Technology in Education**
       480 Charnelton Street • Eugene, OR 97401-2626 USA
Phone: 1.800.336.5191 (U.S. & Canada) • 541.302.3777 (International)

Fax: 541.302.3778
E-mail: orders@iste.org
Web: www.iste.org/bookstore

Use this form to order, or order online at www.iste.org

Name: _____ Membership #: _____

School/Business: _____

Address: _____ City: _____ State: _____

Zip/Postal Code: _____ Country: _____

Code 757

Phone: _____ E-Mail: _____

	Quantity	Membership Order
Join ISTE and its members as we lead the way in preparing students and teachers for the future. ISTE members receive either *Learning & Leading with Technology* or the *Journal of Research on Technology in Education.* ☐ U.S. ($58) ☐ International ($78)	x 1	=

Choose your periodical: ☐ L&L ☐ JRTE (Formerly JRCE)

CALL FOR BULK DISCOUNT PRICING ON THESE TITLES			Quantity	NETS Order
NETS for Students Booklet	☐ Member Price $5.00	☐ Nonmember Price $5.00	x	=
NETS for Students Poster	☐ Member Price $2.95	☐ Nonmember Price $2.95	x	=
NETS for Teachers Booklet	☐ Member Price $13.50	☐ Nonmember Price $15.00	x	=
NETS for Teachers Poster	☐ Member Price $5.00	☐ Nonmember Price $5.00	x	=
NETS for Administrators Booklet	☐ Member Price $13.50	☐ Nonmember Price $15.00	x	=
NETS for Administrators Poster	☐ Member Price $ 5.00	☐ Nonmember Price $ 5.00	x	=

DEDUCT 13% IF ORDERING 10 OR MORE OF ANY SINGLE TITLE BELOW ⟶			Quantity	13% Discount	NETS Order
Connecting Curriculum and Technology	☐ Member Price $26.95	☐ Nonmember Price $29.95	x	-	=
Preparing Teachers to Use Technology	☐ Member Price $44.95	☐ Nonmember Price $49.95	x	-	=
Making Technology Standards Work for You	☐ Member Price $40.45	☐ Nonmember Price $44.95	x	-	=

☐ Payment enclosed. Make checks payable to ISTE— international orders must be prepaid with U.S. funds or credit card.

☐ VISA ☐ MasterCard ☐ Discover Card

☐☐☐☐ ☐☐☐☐ ☐☐☐☐ ☐☐☐☐

Expiration date _____ Signature _____

☐ Purchase Order enclosed. Please add $4.00 for order processing—P.O. not including $4.00 fee will be returned.

☐ Airmail. International orders are sent surface mail— ISTE will bill you the additional shipping charge for airmail.

☐ Send me ISTE membership and subscription information.

SUBTOTAL	=
*Shipping and Handling (see box below)	+
*Add additional 7% of SUBTOTAL if shipped to a PO Box, AK, HI	+
*Add 12% of SUBTOTAL if shipped outside the U.S.	+
Add 7% of SUBTOTAL for GST if shipped to Canada	+
If billed with purchase order, add $4.00	+
NETS ORDER TOTAL	=
MEMBERSHIP ORDER TOTAL	+
TOTAL	=

Order by
Mail: Send this order form to:
International Society for Technology in Education
480 Charnelton Street • Eugene, OR 97401-2626 USA
Phone: 1.800.336.5191 (U.S. & Canada) • 541.302.3777 (International)
Fax: 541.302.3778 • E-mail: orders@iste.org • Web: www.iste.org/bookstore

Photocopy this form for additional memberships.
Prices subject to change without notice.

SHIPPING & HANDLING*

$0–$15.99 (subtotal) . . . . . .add $6.00

$16–$45.99 (subtotal) . . . . .add $7.50

$46–$75.99 (subtotal) . . . . .add $8.50

$76–$119.99 (subtotal) . . . .add $9.50

$120 or more . . . . . . .8% of subtotal

GST Registration Number 128828431

*If actual shipping cost exceeds this amount, we will bill you for the difference.

Use this form to order, or order online at www.iste.org

Name: _____ Membership #: _____

School/Business: _____

Address: _____ City: _____ State: _____

Zip/Postal Code: _____ Country: _____

Code 757

Phone: _____ E-Mail: _____

	Quantity	Membership Order
Join ISTE and its members as we lead the way in preparing students and teachers for the future. ISTE members receive either *Learning & Leading with Technology* or the *Journal of Research on Technology in Education.* ☐ U.S. ($58) ☐ International ($78)	x 1	=
Choose your periodical: ☐ L&L ☐ JRTE (Formerly JRCE)		

CALL FOR BULK DISCOUNT PRICING ON THESE TITLES			Quantity	NETS Order
NETS for Students Booklet	☐ Member Price $5.00	☐ Nonmember Price $5.00	x	=
NETS for Students Poster	☐ Member Price $2.95	☐ Nonmember Price $2.95	x	=
NETS for Teachers Booklet	☐ Member Price $13.50	☐ Nonmember Price $15.00	x	=
NETS for Teachers Poster	☐ Member Price $5.00	☐ Nonmember Price $5.00	x	=
NETS for Administrators Booklet	☐ Member Price $13.50	☐ Nonmember Price $15.00	x	=
NETS for Administrators Poster	☐ Member Price $ 5.00	☐ Nonmember Price $ 5.00	x	=

DEDUCT 13% IF ORDERING 10 OR MORE OF ANY SINGLE TITLE BELOW ⟶			Quantity	13% Discount	NETS Order
Connecting Curriculum and Technology	☐ Member Price $26.95	☐ Nonmember Price $29.95	x	-	=
Preparing Teachers to Use Technology	☐ Member Price $44.95	☐ Nonmember Price $49.95	x	-	=
Making Technology Standards Work for You	☐ Member Price $40.45	☐ Nonmember Price $44.95	x	-	=

☐ Payment enclosed. Make checks payable to ISTE—
international orders must be prepaid with U.S. funds or credit card.

☐ VISA ☐ MasterCard ☐ Discover Card

☐☐☐☐ ☐☐☐☐ ☐☐☐☐ ☐☐☐☐ ☐☐☐

Expiration date _____ Signature _____

☐ Purchase Order enclosed. Please add $4.00 for order processing—P.O. not including $4.00 fee will be returned.
☐ Airmail. International orders are sent surface mail—
ISTE will bill you the additional shipping charge for airmail.
☐ Send me ISTE membership and subscription information.

SUBTOTAL	=
*Shipping and Handling (see box below)	+
*Add additional 7% of SUBTOTAL if shipped to a PO Box, AK, HI	+
*Add 12% of SUBTOTAL if shipped outside the U.S.	+
Add 7% of SUBTOTAL for GST if shipped to Canada	+
If billed with purchase order, add $4.00	+
NETS ORDER TOTAL	=
MEMBERSHIP ORDER TOTAL	+
TOTAL	=

Order by
Mail: Send this order form to:
   International Society for Technology in Education
   480 Charnelton Street • Eugene, OR 97401-2626 USA
Phone: 1.800.336.5191 (U.S. & Canada) • 541.302.3777 (International)
Fax: 541.302.3778 • E-mail: orders@iste.org • Web: www.iste.org/bookstore

Photocopy this form for additional memberships.
Prices subject to change without notice.

SHIPPING & HANDLING*

$0–$15.99 (subtotal) . . . . . .add $6.00

$16–$45.99 (subtotal) . . . . .add $7.50

$46–$75.99 (subtotal) . . . . .add $8.50

$76–$119.99 (subtotal) . . . .add $9.50

$120 or more . . . . . . .8% of subtotal

GST Registration Number 128828431

*If actual shipping cost exceeds this amount, we will bill you for the difference.